"Only the slyest and boldest ... making about music, and families, comes to mind as you read *Low Down*: James Baldwin's 'Sonny's Blues,' or David Goodis's *Down There*. Yet A. J. Albany's spirit and voice are fully her own—fierce, funny, troubling, sad, rueful, joyous."

—ROBERT POLITO

A. J. Albany's recollection of life with her father, the great jazz pianist Joe Albany, is the story of one girl's unsentimental education. Joe played with the likes of Charles Mingus, Lester Young, and Charlie Parker, but between gigs he slipped into drug-induced obscurity. It was during these times that his daughter knew him best. After her mother disappeared, six-year-old Amy Jo and her charming, troubled father set up housekeeping in a seamy Hollywood hotel. While Joe finished a set in some red-boothed dive, chances were you'd find Amy curled up to sleep on someone's fur coat, clutching a 78 of Louis Armstrong's "Sugar Blues" or, later, a photograph of the man himself, inscribed, "To little Amy-Jo, always in love with you—Pops."

Wise beyond her years and hip to the unpredictability of life at all too early an age, A. J. Albany guides us through the dope and deviance of the late 1960s and early 1970s in Hollywood's shadowy underbelly and beyond. What emerges is a raw, gripping, and surprisingly sympathetic portrait of a young girl trying to survive among the outcasts, misfits, and artists who surrounded her.

# LOW DOWN

# LOW DOWN

**junk, jazz, and other
fairy tales from childhood**

*a memoir*

A.J. Albany

 TIN HOUSE BOOKS / Portland, Oregon & Brooklyn, New York

First published by Bloomsbury/Tin House Books in 2003

Published by Tin House Books in 2013

Published by Tin House Books, Portland, Oregon, and
Brooklyn, New York
Distributed to the trade by Publishers Group West, 1700 Fourth
St., Berkeley, CA 94710, www.pgw.com

Library of Congress Cataloging-in-Publication Data

Albany, A. J.
  Low down : junk, jazz, and other fairy tales from childhood /
A.J. Albany.
    pages cm
  ISBN 978-1-935639-76-3
  1. Albany, Joe, 1924-1988. 2. Jazz musicians—United States—
Biography. 3. Pianists—United States—Biography. I. Title.
  ML417.A58A43 2013
  786.2'165092--dc23
  [B]

                              2013024037

First U.S. edition 2003
Printed in the USA
Interior design by Jakob Vala
www.tinhouse.com

For Groucho, Lou Reed, Dovey beloved,
my children, and all children

Special thanks to Jeff Preiss
and Jeanne McCulloch

For each of them has his Preacher to hound him down the dark river of fear and tonguelessness and never-a-door. Each one is mute and alone because there is no word for a child's fear and no ear to heed it if there were a word and no one to understand it if it heard. Lord save little children! They abide and they endure.

—DAVIS GRUBB

And you my father, there on the sad height,
Curse, bless me now with your fierce tears, I pray.

—DYLAN THOMAS

# foreword

Joe Albany was a great jazz pianist. That was the opinion of Charlie Parker, Lester Young, and scores of others who played with him. In the early forties, he was one of the first musicians instrumental in pushing jazz beyond the confines of swing, helping to create what would come to be known as bebop.

I too was in awe of my father's talent, but I loved him all out of proportion, as only a daughter can. He was born in Atlantic City in 1924 and died in New York City in 1988, his body destroyed by half a century of addictions and sadness. In one of his last letters to me he warned, "Watch out for Old Lady Life—she can be an evil bitch."

There has always been an absence of information regarding my father's whereabouts during the sixties. It wasn't a musically productive period for him, but it's when I knew him best. If he wasn't in jail or rehab, we were together. This book is an account of my life with him during that time: a series of fragmented moments seen through the prism of my childhood. It's also a story about growing up and surviving in Hollywood, a rough journey in a unique city that was taking a turn for the worse.

part one

# melody man

I often thought my father was born of music—some wayward melody that took the form of a man. He heard music
everywhere, in the squeaking of rusted bedsprings and the
buzzing of flies. Dripping faucets were filled with rhythms
to him, as was the irregular flashing of the busted neon outside our window. Some shook their heads and thought he
was a nut, but I never believed that. He'd play recordings
of Art Tatum, Arthur Rubenstein, and others, and exclaim
with flashing eyes, "What a gas—beauteous!" Sometimes
we'd listen to records all night. When legit gigs weren't available, Dad did short stints in hotel bars, where his exquisite
playing was often underappreciated, to say the least. It was
always the same type who caused trouble—an out-of-town
drunk with a tin ear, usually in the company of some flabby
lounge whore. They'd stumble over to the piano, leaning on
the keys, and say something like, "How about using that soft
pedal, pal?" or "Do you know this one?" and proceed to whis-
tle some corny number, spitting smelly off-tune whistles in
Dad's ear. He'd take it on the chin every time, never uttering
a word, but I, who knew him, would see his spirit wilt just
behind the eyes. When I sensed his hurt, I'd imagine that

I was the Abominable Dr. Phibes, devising fiendish deaths for these bar stool critics, or I'd transform into Rodan, grabbing my victims by their fat red necks with razor talons. I'd fly them to an underground vault where I, now the masked executioner, waited, ready to end the lives of fools and hecklers everywhere who didn't know beauty when they heard it.

## soft downy dreams

The day that Gram gave birth to her eleven-pound, colicky son Joe, January 24, 1924, was the beginning of a sad voyage for them both. At the age of seventeen, Gram was a lover of life. She loved dancing and was a founder of the As You Like It club, a group of South Philly girls who shared a passion for literature. Unlike today's book clubs, where women get together and usually read a lot of slop, Gram and her friends got together and read truly great books: Dostoyevsky, Balzac, the Brontës, all the Romantic poets.

At the age of eighteen, she met August Albani. So flattered was she by the overtures of "Gus" the traveling citrus salesman that she ran off and married him, much to the dismay of her parents. Being a virgin of the purest order, she was shocked to discover that a man's member was not covered in soft downy fur, as she had thought. Though sex is usually a letdown when compared to the fantasies available to one's imagination, Gram was devastated to find the experience so utterly unpleasurable.

I have no kind words for my grandfather, though it could be argued that his fierce determination served to help his children excel musically, producing two fine pianists and an opera singer. Himself a frustrated tenor of limited ability, Grandpop would settle for nothing short of perfection from his kids, driving them to practice their instruments for hours on end.

As a young man, he allowed a local wealthy pervert to shit in his mouth, for a price. Perhaps this incident was why a lot of foul things came out of his mouth. He would beat Gram, and my father too, whenever he dared to intervene. Dad contended that Grandpop had uprooted the family from their New Jersey home and moved to L.A. in 1941 for the sole purpose of separating Dad from his high school sweetheart, Joyce. Joyce was a Jewish girl, which was more than my grandpop's bigoted heart could bear. One day, a few years later, when Dad brought Charlie Parker home for supper, Grandpop turned to Dad and said, "Get this nigger out of my house." After such woeful beginnings, life offered my father talent as a consolation prize, but it was like giving tap shoes to an amputee. He had immense talent but lacked the ability to enjoy it.

After arriving in L.A., Dad attended Hollywood High School for six months before growing sick of it and dropping out. He'd already decided on a career in music, and in the summer of '42 he headed back to Atlantic City to begin pursuing it. While there, he played for a while at a place called the Paddock Club, where the headlining act was a female snake charmer named Zorita. Hearing that L.A.'s Central Avenue had blossomed into a hotbed of jazz, he bused back to Hollywood in 1944. It was then that he met his first wife, B.J., who Grandpop referred to only as "that painted she-devil." Their brief marriage was a casualty of impetuous youth. In 1945 two pivotal events happened to Dad that would dictate the course of his life. The first was his meeting and playing with Charlie Parker, and the second was his introduction to heroin. From that point on, his music and his addictions would battle endlessly to see which would prevail.

## escaping camarillo

At the age of twenty-two, Dad underwent a psychiatric evaluation while serving time on drug charges. He was diagnosed with hebephrenia, a form of schizophrenia that manifests itself in puberty and is characterized by unprovoked laughter, foolish mannerisms, and delusions. Grandpop signed the commitment papers, and Dad was sent to Camarillo State Hospital.

Doctors, being somewhat in the dark back then about the treatment of drug addicts, prescribed endless mugs of hot chocolate and warm baths, which did little to soothe his troubled psyche. Not considered dangerous, he was placed with patients suffering from epilepsy and was expected to help out hospital staff in the event of any seizures that might occur.

By odd coincidence, Charlie Parker had been committed to Camarillo a short time earlier, after being found wandering around naked in a Los Angeles hotel corridor. Parker spotted Dad standing in an upper window as he walked in the yard below. He waved to him and sent a guy up with some chocolate Sucrets, cigarettes, and a note saying, "Joe— see you when you get into population—Bird." Dad, however, had already determined not to hang around. He had a girlfriend on the outside, and figured in his usual paranoid manner that she was up to no good. While standing naked in line for a medical exam that was required before one could be released into "population," he made his move. He broke out of line, headed straight out the door with his clothes in his hands, and jumped over the barbed-wire fence. Unfortunately, Camarillo would not be his last visit to a nuthouse, and future visits would see his treatments graduate from hot cocoa to shock therapy.

Aside from being eccentric and supersensitive, I don't think there was anything wrong with Dad. Society was of the mind that one "had to be crazy" if they chose to take drugs, and doctors were probably under a certain amount of pressure to back this sentiment up with medical evidence, readily labeling addicts as mental cases. The diagnosis of hebephrenia would always haunt my father. Known for doodling on everything in sight, he would write *hebephrenic* over and over on scraps of paper, sheet music, and matchbook covers for the rest of his life.

# belle of salt lake city

It was said by those who knew her that my mother, Sheila, was "the Belle of Salt Lake City," where she was born on St. Patrick's Day, 1932. She was afforded such niceties as dance classes and piano lessons, and her IQ was said to be 165. Her great-great-great-uncle, I've been told, was the poet John Keats.

Our time together was brief. Most of what I know of her is what I've read and what my dad told me. A lot of that information concerned her relationship with the late poet Allen Ginsberg. They had met around '56 or '57, and Ginsberg was struck by what he called her "classy good looks" and vast knowledge of music and books, especially for a twenty-two-year-old gal from Utah. Mom was working at an advertising firm in San Francisco, writing copy, and hooked Ginsberg up with a job there doing the same. They shared an apartment on Russian Hill and for some brief period of time maintained a life together, with Mom riding the hills of San Francisco on the back of Ginsberg's motorcycle. At one point, they announced that they were engaged, which went over badly with William Burroughs, who was appalled at the very idea of Ginsberg being involved with a woman. Occasionally, they'd show up at the home of my mother's sister, where Ginsberg enjoyed raiding the well-stocked liquor cabinet. When Mom's brother-in-law returned home from work one day and found Ginsberg finishing off a bottle of his best Irish whiskey, he flipped. "Get the hell out of here, you good-for-nothing bum." Mom burst into tears, saying, "How can you talk to him like that? Don't you know he's a genius?" It seemed she was crazy about him, and a letter that he wrote to Jack Kerouac indicated likewise: "I met a great girl who digs me, I dig—twenty-two, young, hip (ex-singer, big buddy of Brubeck, knows all the colored cats, ex-hipster girl) pretty in a real chic classy way—she has a wild mind, finer than any girl I met . . .—young life in her and real sharp. What a doll . . . Not a stupid square in any way, but not a flip. Instant digging each other—how wild and great." Ginsberg wrote an unpublished poem for her entitled "In Vesuvio's Waiting for Sheila."

However, Ginsberg soon grew disenchanted and wrote Kerouac another letter complaining that Mom was "Younger and more prey to psychological semi-dramatizations. Sheila says I'm an abstractionist and not a Dostoievskian lover." The first time I heard a recording of Kerouac reading *On the Road*, I thought it was my father. Though Dad's accent was New Jersey and Kerouac's Massachusetts, they had the same reedy, rambling voice, with the same slightly nervous cadence. I always thought Dad's dentures had something to do with his not always clear speaking. Not knowing Kerouac's dental history, I couldn't say whether my theory could be applied to him.

In the late seventies, Ginsberg ran into my dad walking down Bleecker Street in New York, and upon recognizing him, grabbed his arm, exclaiming, "It's the great Joe Albany!" Jazz musicians were always flattered and somewhat

mystified over the lofty status lent them by the Beat writ-
ers, who viewed bebop musicians as inspirational gurus and
made them the subject of much poetry and prose. In the
course of conversation, Ginsberg asked Dad, "Did I ever
tell you how Sheila and I parted ways? I came home one
day and told her I was in love with someone else, and when
she asked who, I said it was Neal Cassady. She kicked me
out." I gather Mom was Ginsberg's last heterosexual li-
aison. It figures that Ginsberg would cite Cassady as the
catalyst in their breakup. The three of them had apparently
slept together on several occasions. Ginsberg also con-
fessed to my dad that "Sheila helped write some of the best
lines in *Howl*."

Sometime after the breakup, Mom, drunk and despon-
dent, went to the apartment that Ginsberg was sharing
with Peter Orlovsky and pelted the window with bottles
and rocks, yelling, "You can fuck me in the ass, if that's
what it's all about!" It was also rumored that Mom lived
with Henry Miller for a spell, but that's never been verified. I always assumed that there wasn't much truth in what
she said, though the factuality of her tales never seemed
that important. The only truth that mattered, to me, was
that there was the potential for all of it to be true, and then
some. It was her sterling potential that inspired my admi-
ration. She had all the makings of someone truly great.

# meeting

My parents met in 1959 at one of pianist Erroll Garner's parties in L.A. Dad and Erroll were pretty close, and when I was born, he asked to be my godfather, but some Italian guy named Frank Perry was already in place for that position. I had a favorite picture of myself on top of Mr. Garner's shoulders. He was a kind and gentle man.

My mother walked into the party, and someone let her know that Joe Albany was at the piano, which set her bohemian heart a-flutter, since her favorite album at that time was *The Right Combination*, Dad's collaboration with saxophonist Warne Marsh, which had been released in 1957—the only record Dad made before the 1970s. Funny to think of jazz musicians generating that sort of rock-star excitement among women. She made her way over to the piano and introduced herself as an aspiring jazz singer. He asked her if she knew "Our Love Is Here to Stay"—naturally, she did. At some point, as she was singing, she looked at him and his head was down on the keyboard, and he was shaking, she assumed, with laughter. She told him, "Look, I know I'm no Billie Holiday, but it can't be that bad." Then she realized that he was sobbing. He explained that "Our Love Is Here to Stay" was his and his second wife Aileen's song, and that she had recently committed suicide. Aileen was tragic. Unbalanced, and always threatening to kill herself, one night she said to Dad, "I'm really going to do it this time, I'm going to run in front of the next car I see."

He replied, "Sure you are—why don't you stop torturing me?" It was the last thing he'd say to her—a second later, before he knew what was happening, she bolted in front of an oncoming truck. He tried to grab her, but it was too late. She died in his arms.

Mom and Dad soon embarked on their ill-advised love affair. Sheila dumped the young drummer that she'd been shacked up with and pregnant by, had the baby, and gave her up for adoption to a childless couple in the Bay Area. One week later, on St. Patrick's Day, 1960, my mother's twenty-eighth birthday, she and Dad were married in San Francisco. They rented a small apartment in Hollywood and fixed it up with the money Mom made from the adoption. I came along in February of 1962—I'd like to think it was a happy occasion, though all the track marks on her arms in pictures where she's holding me make me wonder. I know that Dad had wanted a girl, and I looked just like him, so I guess he was pleased. My mother named me after two of the sisters in *Little Women*, Amy, the feminine one, and Jo, the bookish tomboy, hoping I'd possess the qualities of both sisters. Dad described the night I was conceived as a "particularly passionate moment" in a relationship full of great passion and greater sorrow. When together, they seemed to bring out the worst in each other, always competing to see who could fall the fastest and the furthest down the ladder to hell.

# ace-one-boon-white-coon

Dad told me that when I was an infant, Dizzy Gillespie dropped me on my head. It was a fact that always disturbed him greatly. He'd say, "Well, maybe he was stoned, but I think he was just trying to show off." I never understood what that meant—seemed a strange way to show off, dropping a baby. Either way, it always bugged him. He said he never trusted Dizzy after that, which I choose to take as a sign of parental love. I've often wondered if this incident was the reason I've never been a big Dizzy Gillespie fan.

I'm not certain if this is a first memory, or if I simply heard my dad tell the story so often that it feels like memory. In the summer of '63 I was living with my parents in Harlem. Dad was playing at the Village Gate with Charles Mingus. He would later tell me that it was "a real sweatbox" playing with Mingus, and referred to the gig as "ten days of Sodom and Gomorrah." Dad was also the only ofay in the group, which created its own brand of tension. One day we were walking down the street, passing a newsstand, when I stopped to pick up a magazine, maybe *Life*, with Thelonious Monk on the cover. I kissed it, and said, "Hi, Monk." Dad, combusting with pride, picked me up and looked at me with his beautiful gray-green eyes and said, "From now on you're not just my baby, you're my ace-one-boon-white-coon." That, he would claim, was the day we forever connected, and became more to each other than everything.

# dolls and great winged men

Blood. Its distinct shade of red stays vivid even in memories that have long faded into shadow. I remember standing at the bars of a crib around the age of two, disturbed over fighting that was raging in another room. My mother came in, turned on the light, and staggered toward me, whispering, "Hush now. No more crying." As she reached in the crib to lay me back down, I saw that her neck was covered with blood. It trickled onto my cherished baby doll that was dressed in a fleecy rabbit costume. I don't recall being aware of any other colors aside from the bright blood that stood out like liquid poppies on snow against my mother's long white neck. Somehow the sight of this silenced me. I lay next to my splattered doll and stared at it, unblinking. All sounds were distant now. A few days later, Mom said, "Oh look—you've gotten ketchup on your doll." Perhaps I'd dreamt the whole thing. I thought it best to get rid of the doll in an attempt to forget the incident, but her discarded spirit called to me from the dark earth. The doll's absence only intensified my memory of her. She was another fallen soldier of the drug wars, powerless and unlucky, with friends like herself buried all over town.

It was around the same time I lost my doll that the Great Winged Man first appeared to me. He was born, I suppose, out of despair, though I felt certain that he was real, for he'd never come to me when I attempted to conjure him—only when I was beaten down and no one was near me to witness it. It was then that he'd approach me, always from behind, and pick me up with huge, black, batlike wings that covered me completely. He'd place me on his warm, levitating lap, where I was lulled into a gentle sleep. On occasion, I tried to capture a glimpse of his face. Once I managed to shift my head upward, out of the balled-up position his wings held me tightly in, and saw the smile of Louis Armstrong, and my father's gray-green eyes looking down at me. He was my sympathetic demon superhero. There were times when I was weak with hunger and I felt certain he was Death come to carry me away. Instead he arrived to save me. The Great Winged Man hid me away and provided a safe place to sleep.

## some other "halves"

Between my mother and father, I have an alleged total of eight half siblings who have shown up so far. Each of my mom's five children has a different father.

Most of my half siblings on my father's side have inherited all of the sad vulnerability and unrest that comes with our father's genes. My half brother, Joe Jr., has been institutionalized for most of his adult life, a paranoid schizophrenic, so they say. When I first met him I was fourteen years old. He must have been twenty-four or twenty-five. No one would allow him to finish his own sentences, a nervous habit that people often exercise around those they deem "not right in the head." Acute sensitivity was the only thing Joe suffered from, as far as I could see. He's too gentle for this world. My half sister, pretty and sharp tongued, enjoyed a good time, maybe too much so. That was years ago.

For the past fourteen years, Dad has resided in a paint can toward the back of my closet. It's not a scenic resting place, but it's peaceful, and I've grown fond of having him nearby, though I'd originally intended to scatter his ashes in Paris, his favorite city. Another good reason for keeping him close is the fact that they can get DNA out of cremated remains. When the next somebody comes forward claiming to have been sired by Dad, I'll give them a nickel bag of ashes and suggest they have a lab check them out before the family reunion begins. "Gee, was he really a jazz musician? What was his favorite color? Hey, that's a coincidence. I feel like I know him already." It's as if I'd waited patiently to get on a ride, standing in a long, unending queue, only to have someone cut in front of the line. They put in no time, didn't even buy a ticket. Being an only child, I don't like to share, and once on that ride, I'm not keen to let anyone have a go.

## snapshots

Sometimes, I feel I'm on the verge of remembering something. It only happens when certain elements are in place. It's always at dusk, at the end of a warm day, when there's a breeze—enough to flutter thin curtains—and I'm lying on my side, looking out the window. It's then that something tries to come to me, but never quite does. Mostly, it's about the air—the air has a particular hazy quality that makes the sadness come. Then there's the sense of waiting. I'm waiting calmly for something that I've grown not to fear. Perhaps when the time is right—if ever—I'll remember.

One summer afternoon when I was four and the air was moving expectantly, two men came to take away our furniture, including my dad's piano. He wasn't home, but Mom was sitting on the porch in a rocking chair, close to the edge of the stairs. One of the men asked her to move, but she wouldn't—only sat there with the faintest smile, serene as the Buddha. The man picked up the chair and dumped her down the stairs, as if emptying out a pail of water. Her head cracked open and blood flowed down the pavement, but her expression never changed. Men kept moving out furniture, just stepping over her like a slight imposition. "Goddamn junkies," one of them said. I thought she was dead and I ran and ran, down the street to nowhere. It fades to black after that—like all my snapshot memories.

## sleeping in bars

For a time in 1966, Dad maintained a regular gig at a bar in Hollywood. It was your classic dark, red-boothed, booze-drenched dive, warm and inviting to my four-year-old eyes. I would sit there each night with Daphne, a ravishing red-haired hooker, Martino the bartender, and a number of other regulars who kept an eye on me while Dad played his set. Dad referred to one particular group of four regulars as "the Hard-Luck Charlie Club." They were all ex-vaudevillians of one sort or another; I know one man had been a hoofer for sure, because he taught me how to do a stomping triple-time step. The only woman in the group had done some act with a snake and a chimp that wasn't clear to me at the time, though I knew she'd gotten arrested in Idaho Falls for "lewd acts." "All for the love of some bum," she'd say. Her bemoaning became more pronounced with each pink lady she polished off. I didn't care for her because she took to berating Dad for exposing me to "degenerate riffraff," herself included, I'm sure. Dad muttered that she was an "old hag chimp fucker" and henceforth refused to play her nightly request of "Polka Dots and Moonbeams." "It's a dumb-ass song anyway," he said. I myself drank too many Shirley Temples with red and green cherries and listened to dirty jokes I didn't get until years later. At some point, I'd be hoisted up on the piano, and I dutifully sang and danced to "Satin Doll" or "All of Me." Around eleven o'clock I'd fall asleep and was placed behind the bar, usually on someone's fur coat, until midnight, when Dad finished work. In the morning it was my duty to count the tips that Dad had collected in the large brandy glass the night before. It was good early math education. When Dad's habit wasn't getting the best of him, he really tried to keep us together.

# the pickled pool

I remember very little between the ages of two and five, though I don't suppose many people do. Yet I do remember knowing instinctively that school would always be a source of great unhappiness for me, a parallel hell away from home. And so it was, beginning with my first—and last—day of nursery school. After my screams had subsided into jagged sobs of defeat, Dad left me in the hands of two women who must have been trained at the Charles Dickens School of Child Abuse. I was told to get in the sandbox and play, which I did for a total of thirty seconds before some lug of a kid shoved half a bucket of sand in my mouth. A teacher dangled me over the drinking fountain, commanding me to rinse, asking why, after only five minutes, I was already getting into trouble.

I thought of a song I loved to play at home—"Look for the Silver Lining," which I'd always assumed was sung by someone's sexy young mother until Dad introduced me to Chet Baker one day and told me he was the singer on the album that I so admired. Thinking of it always helped a little. I tried to keep a low profile, after checking the gate and realizing that escape was out of the question. That place was "buttoned up tighter than a spinster's snatch," as Dad used to say. Lunchtime came, and of all the possible edibles in the universe, they served fish sticks, the very smell of which triggered my delicate gag reflex. A teacher was soon by my side looking dismayed at the sight of my untouched plate. "Start eating, young lady."

"But I feel sick," I replied, sincerely, as I felt grains of sand still grating between my teeth. "You'll sit here until you eat," she said firmly. A kid across the table from me was proudly displaying an open mouth filled with congealed fish. Breathing carefully through my nose, I picked one up and bit the smallest-ever bite off the end. I suddenly felt a cavalry charging up from my stomach's pit and into my throat and then threw up with a force so great that all who witnessed it fell silent, except for the teacher, who made some strange, indistinguishable noise.

After cleaning up, I was permitted to lie down on a mat for the rest of the day. It was a brown vinyl mat that felt cool against my cheek. I left my eyes half opened. Since they were watery—my eyes always watered when I was sick—the sunlight through the windows streamed in like long, golden ribbons, pixilating with the moving air. The sound of kids taunting each other faded away, and I floated up, up, over the gates and into a bizarre dream that I remember vividly. In this dream, I was dancing with a jar of mustard around a pool that was filled with pickle juice. I loved pickle juice, drank it out of the jar. That and mustard had helped me survive on a least one occasion. Music played on, cares were none, and just as I was about to dive in for a swim, I heard my father's voice: "Jo-Jo, hey." I awoke feeling as though I'd spent a hundred years sleeping on the moon and could no longer function in the human race. It felt fine.

Dad carried me home on his shoulders, saying that the teachers didn't think I was ready for school yet. Now my contentment was complete. In time, however, I'd find out that my vomiting capabilities would not be enough to keep me out of school forever. The future would call for more drastic measures.

## three mother tales

I.

By the age of five, I was acutely aware that my life could be snuffed out in an instant. Never was this feeling stronger than when I was left in the hands of my lovely mother. Mom was petite and fair, with blue-green cat eyes—"Eyes you would happily drown in," Dad used to say.

Among Mom's talents was an uncanny ability to forge signatures. It would land her in the glasshouse three times. Her favorite thing to forge was medical prescriptions, and the drug she most prescribed for herself was Dilaudid. She would spend days on end semiconscious, falling off toilets, not one motherly bone in her whole beautiful body—a fact that sort of impressed me, on some twisted level. I learned early to fend for myself, foraging for food like some small, freaked-out animal. When real food wasn't available, I'd invent new things to eat. Shaving cream, toothpaste, and some pink, supposedly poisonous berries that grew on a bush outside our door.

I wasn't the healthiest kid around, but I survived, which, I guess, is a good thing. I decided to make a short list in my mind of the essentials. Besides food, there was the record player for pleasure and drowning out unpleasant sounds, and there was sleep. To sleep, I needed pajamas, and I was very fond of my flannel PJs—I felt safe with them on. One night, unable to locate them and with my mother out of her head in a Dilaudid haze, I ventured out into the Hollywood courtyard where we lived and started knocking on neighbors' doors for some assistance. Since it was midnight and I was all of five years old and half naked, one would assume that a friendly face might emerge from behind a blank door—but that was not the case. It was my first lesson in humanity. Terrified women peeked out from their curtains, shooing me away. My parents had developed a reputation as the local lunatic druggies who played music at all hours, and I was simply their demon spawn. So there I sat, in the middle of our courtyard, on the edge of an old broken fountain that featured a lonely, armless cherub being strangled by weeds. The courtyard seemed huge. It was black out and freezing, a very pathetic scene. Dad was playing at the jazz club called Pepys on Sunset Strip and got home around 3:00 AM. When he saw me waiting there, he snapped, ran into the house, and smacked Mom around. I felt some sadness for her, but not too much. At least he woke her up, and I was able to get to sleep, properly attired, and dream that I was a thousand miles away from my life. I formed a lot of opinions that night that live with me, for better or for worse, like tiny devils. I hate the dark and the cold and the sense of empty space around me. I have no faith in most people, particularly women, but I'm fond of coconut-lime shaving cream.

## II.

Mom would appear and disappear as often as the sun on a cloudy day. By the age of five, I went to great lengths attempting to endear myself to her. I turned into a pathetic court jester trying to avoid getting the ax from an unamused queen.

Despite my efforts, every few months she'd depart, until I felt like the discarded result of a failed experiment and eventually grew weary of the whole situation. At the best of times, she'd dip her toe into the dark waters of motherhood and briefly display a distracted affection, ever looking over her shoulder for either her connection or her misspent youth.

Mom was around when I was invited to the fifth-birthday party of a girl named Sherry who lived two courtyards down. The usual festivities were commencing: pinning of donkey tails and duck-duck-goosing, but I had difficulty entering into the spirit of things and fell back on my unconscious habit of picking my nose and eating its contents. For some reason, I was recalling a picture I'd seen of Joan of Arc that had made me very sad. The picture was in a children's encyclopedia I'd found in a neighbor's trash can. It showed young Joan being burned at the stake while a crowd of onlookers stood by and jeered. Her expression was calm and graceful, and her face looked toward heaven as she accepted and transcended her fate. I was entering the deep state of daydream where all outside sound dissipates when a fellow partygoer gave me a nudge and my thoughts were shattered. I looked around to see an army of vicious young eyes bearing down on me, laughing hysterically. I was busted. I took off running for home with the vermin in hot pursuit, a scene from *Lord of the Flies*. As I ran through the door in tears, crying for my mother, I found her unconscious on the floor, naked and facedown in her vomit. I sat cross-legged and thought for a moment. This wasn't a new scene, certainly, but she was chillingly still and unnatural in color. My stomach growled—I'd left the party before the cake serving—and my finger once again went for my nose.

There was an old Japanese gardener I'd noticed working next door. Maybe he would help. Pulling an old plaid blanket from the couch, I covered her up, and after much tugging and gesturing, the reluctant gardener came to my aid. Upon seeing my mother on the floor, he began jumping around like a man who'd stepped into a school of jellyfish. I suddenly thought of Jerry Lewis impersonating a Chinese guy, since this gardener came complete with buck teeth and a bamboo sun hat. As he called for an ambulance, I ran off to hide and lie in wait until my father returned home. Mom was in the hospital for a week, then went to San Francisco to recuperate. I assume she took a cure of some kind, though I don't know any specifics. When she wasn't around, I gained much attention from my dad, and if he worked, I'd usually go to the home of my grandmother, where I'd drink egg coffee, which was coffee mixed with a beaten yolk, sugar, and hot milk, and sit by the radiator, contented.

When Mom returned, I felt somewhat disappointed, though everyone else treated it like a blessed event. Years later, Dad said: "Your mother nearly died that day," to which my only reaction was: "Oh." She died each time she took off. After the first few times, it was a phantom who returned to me, its image growing dimmer with each return.

III.

One Sunday, Mom took me to the park, along with two goofballs chased down by a bottle of Ripple. She was perfectly elegant when she passed out. She would fall with grace and pick herself up like a queen who'd fallen off her throne. Halfway through the park, she was facedown in a little stream. My biggest fear was that the water spiders might attack her, so I tried to pull her out, but I was a skinny kid and it was to no avail. When a man walking by stopped and asked, "Is that your mom, kid? Are you all right?" I decided to simply sit by her trying to look carefree.

"Yeah, we're fine, thanks—she's resting," I said with shaky authority. Previous experiences had made me reluctant to ask for help. The man left but looked suspicious, and I started really shaking her, saying that the police were on their way, which got a slight response out of her. After a seemingly endless amount of time, she started to shift, and was finally able to make it to her feet. Somehow we made it back home. That evening, Mom confided: "When you were born, I could see you were Joe's baby and not some trick's kid, so I decided to keep you." One week later, she left without a word. I was five years old, and it would be years before I'd see her again.

part two

# pops

It was in late 1967 that my father worked with the great Louis Armstrong. I'd been a big fan since infancy, according to my dad, who said I'd laugh and dance madly the second I heard the gravelly voice of Satchmo. At five, I slept with a 78 of "Sugar Blues"—or maybe it was "Sugar Foot Strut"—that was pressed on blue vinyl.

So it was arranged that I would accompany Dad to work one night to meet my hero. I can't remember where this club was. It was more of a hall, really, bright and big, and when we walked inside, it was wall-to-wall people. Dad, at six feet, looked over the top of this crowd, spotted Mr. Armstrong, and pushed us through toward the front. Everyone started to part, like in a movie, and looked down at me, a sea of smiling faces that made me all the more nervous. As the last few people moved aside, there he sat on a chair, looking straight at me with a bigger-than-huge smile, arms outstretched. "You must be little Jo I've heard so much about," he said, drawing me to him. I corrected him that my name was Amy Jo—I was always embarrassed by my dad's litany of nicknames. "Well, *Miss* Amy Jo, I've got a song that's just about you," at which point he stood me directly in front of him while my dad got on the piano—I'm afraid I can't recall the other musicians—and started to sing the verse to "Once in Love with Amy." I was frozen. I kept staring at his knees. Here was this man, better than Santa or God to me, singing my song. I almost blacked out—just kept concentrating on his kneecaps, too terrified to blink. Afterward, he gave me a hug and a sloppy kiss, and I stayed there until I fell asleep that night. Two days later, Dad gave me an autographed picture: "To little Amy-Jo, always in love with you—Pops." That became my new item to sleep with, right up to the day it mysteriously disappeared. It probably found its way to the pawnshop.

## visiting day

In January 1968, Dad played out and did a three-month stretch at CRC—California Rehabilitation Center in Corona. Every couple of weeks, one of my father's two sisters would drive my grandmother and me out to visit him. When I was young, my aunts' glamour, as I perceived it, was the stuff of movies. They were a symphony of shiny jewels, bright lips, and voluptuous décolleté. Between the long drive and the dueling perfumes that competed for space in the airtight car, I'd spend the whole trip throwing up and dry-heaving into a beige plastic bucket that was provided for just such occasions.

The prison garb at CRC was all denim, with dark blue denim button-down shirts. There was a large visiting room

with round tables and slick Formica floors, great for sliding across. Dad seemed to find religion during this time, at
least partly because access to the center's piano was through
the pastor. One of his strange, often beautiful letters to me
began, "Darling Daughter, may the great and gentle savior
smile on you, and His divine hand touch you with benevo-
lence and benediction." It sounded like he was tripping.

Visiting days were my singular source of joy, and the best
part of these visits—next to seeing Dad—were my encounters with the vending machines. There were at least ten
vending machines that dispensed everything imaginable,
the most impressive being a cocoa machine that gave you
the option of ordering plain, with marshmallows, or "extra
rich," whatever that meant, and you could see it being made
through a tiny magic window. While I emptied handfuls of
dimes into the machines—stocking up for the pukefest on
the ride home—Dad would sit with his mom and a sister,
listening distractedly to the latest news, hands folded on the
table, head of soft curls nodding slowly. I'd look at him, ad-
miring his strong, straight mouth, Roman nose of distinc-
tion, and overcast colored eyes that always caught mine, and
when they did, something lovely would pass between us. I'd
go home and cry to think of it and spend much of my life
looking for that connection with someone else.

For the three months Dad was at CRC, I lived with
my grandmother. Gram was born Angela Stella Cecelia
LaRocca in Philadelphia in 1903, first-generation Sicilian and Calabrese. We lived in a duplex on Wilton Place

between Franklin Avenue and Hollywood Boulevard, and I attended school when I was well enough, but usually I was sick, battling chronic asthma.

One consolation was the stereo. I was holding on to Dad's records for him. I also had a book on Greek mythology with great, gory pictures in it that I must have read twenty times. It was a comfort to read about the gods and goddesses who suffered far worse than I did—Cronus eating his children, et cetera. It more than compensated for my prior shaving cream consumption. I'd marvel as Gram's old able hands rolled out sheets of fresh pasta for ravioli that were so thin you could see through them. She even made her own sausages and let me crank the meat into the casing. She could combine three simple ingredients—tomato, garlic, and olive oil—and turn them into something worth living for. "Time," she'd say, "is the secret. You can't rush cooking. That and a good iron pan."

At night we'd sit together on her old olive green sofa and I'd listen to sad tales of missed opportunities with "good guys" from her past who she could have, should have married instead of Grandpop, who she usually referred to as "the jerk who couldn't even dance." Sometimes Gram would put on a record and we'd dance to an Italian mazurka or "The Lady in Red." She'd take out the Ouija board and make it move, I swear to God, without even touching it. Strong, sad, loyal, and leagues above everybody, Gram was a martyred saint. The only woman I ever loved.

# the witch of wilton place

Gram had a real bona fide witch in her neighborhood named Grace Moon. Though most of the kids crossed the street to avoid her old, ivy-strangled craftsman house, I was drawn to it like a magnet. Exotic smells and great music always wafted out through her open door, and she had many friendly cats. I'd been obsessed with the possibility of modern-day witches, particularly lovely ones, ever since seeing the movie *Bell, Book, and Candle*.

For a while, I just milled around the front porch playing with her pet Siamese, Beelzebub, until one day she invited me in for a cup of nasty-tasting tea. I was bowled over by her record collection, which she said belonged to her old man, who was serving three years in Chino Prison for some undisclosed crime. Grace was nice, but she was on junk, and it crossed my mind that she might know Dad, since they shared a common interest. I came to understand later that most addicts were solitary souls. They were too paranoid and entrenched in the business of securing their next fix to be bothered with socializing. It was a hard and crooked road to travel.

At Grace's house, I would sit and listen to the Stones' *Out of Our Heads* a hundred times over, and it never seemed to faze her. I knew from experience with my dad when it was all right to speak, and when the sound of my or anyone else's voice would be as welcome as a mouthful of rusty nails. My mother had read palms, tarot cards, the stars, and whatever else struck her fancy, but Grace added spell books, rituals, and potions made from dragons' blood and bats' balls into the mix, which was terribly exciting to a kid like myself, hell-bent on escaping her life.

Mrs. Broad, the old fossil living to Grace's left, was known by all to be a mean dose of trouble who hated just about everything. After she proudly announced one morning that she had poisoned Grace's favorite cat Spooky for entering her yard, Grace cast a mighty spell on her. Five days after the incident, word spread that Mrs. Broad had miraculously contracted oral gonorrhea. The hygienic Mrs. Broad, who'd been a lifelong spinster with a frigid disdain for human contact, was now relegated to a life of antibiotics and peroxide gargles. Grace took credit for it, and I for one wasn't going to argue with her. Once I asked why she didn't consider casting a spell on herself that would end her heroin habit. She looked at me with eyes that were jewels from a sunken treasure. "I have no desire to stop." Until then, that possibility never occurred to me.

Once Grace's husband was released, we lost touch. Now the door was always locked, the heavy black curtains were drawn, and even the cats were kept inside. Grace was stricken from my memory in the usual expedient way I'd become accustomed to. The trick was to keep enough distance between yourself and all the transitory unreliables you'd meet from the get-go. It was the only way to handle the disappointment that came when they invariably decided to dismiss you.

# koko

After Dad's release, we moved into the St. Francis Hotel on Hollywood Boulevard, just west of Western. It was a nondescript four-story brick building with a large lobby and small rooms that housed a vast assortment of misfits. It's where we would reside, periodically, over the next few years.

There was a fire escape just outside our window at the St. Francis. Fire escapes are sublime. I spent endless days and nights out there, watching madness and nothing at all, from the safety of three stories up. The old Hollywood House of Billiards was catty-corner to the hotel. I loved to watch the sharp-looking hustlers with alligator cue cases, and the not-so-sharp suckers who'd get drunk and grifted, come and go. The corner of Hollywood and Western was always alive.

If the fire escape was my sanctuary, then staying in the care of Koko the clown was my damnation. Dad wasn't working too much around this time, and his habit started raging. However, his reputation did land him the occasional job. Some of his gigs were in hardcore titty bars, which was both sad and demeaning for a musician of his caliber. It was during these seedy jobs that I would be left with our friendly neighbor Koko, who—according to him—had been Barnum and Bailey's biggest circus star back in the day. Koko was bald except for a few tufts of orange hair. His eyes were the mad eyes of a ferret, and his skin was shiny and pink. He had no eyebrows and reminded me of the sideshow geek in *Nightmare Alley*. He did a lot of mescaline, if I remember right, and he made me a very nervous six-year-old.

Koko had lots of little games he liked to play, like Find Mr. Elephant—a can-you-grab-the-elephant's-trunk (i.e., his dick) kind of game. He could never get me to do it. I was a fairly sharp kid and just sat in silent repulsion while he squealed and jumped around, basically got himself off. To his credit, he never hurt me, never forced me into anything. I think he adored me, in his own way. He would always bring me little broken toys he'd found and make up songs: "A.J. is an angel bright who lights up Koko clownie's night." I never told my father about Koko's game—I knew Dad would kill him if he found out, and then I'd really be screwed. A year later, Koko threw himself over a freeway overpass and died. Dad was hesitant to tell me. Over dinner one night he said, "Koko has gone away, A.J., but he liked you very much." Indeed he did.

## magic gizmo

Trying to look out for yourself at all of six years old can be a brain-twisting experience. Sometimes I'll walk by a kid now and be able to tell immediately, that's where their life is at. You can recognize it in the hard way they set their face, and in the eyes, at once empty and wise, ready to weep and tell you to fuck off at any time. I look at them and see myself as a kid.

Joy in its various forms is strictly a luxury item. There's no room for frivolous thoughts when your stomach is empty and the next day is an uncertainty. Ever watchful and cautious, you're on the lookout for cops, molesters, shopkeepers, landlords, and all the "well-intentioned" adults who are full of concern only when their schedule allows. Now and then someone comes along, dangling a candy apple full of false hope and poison in your face, and for an instant your battered wisdom is knocked unconscious by the possibility of a proper meal or soft pillow. Crazy as it sounds, at times one kind smile in your direction is all it takes. Suddenly your guard is down, and you abandon your credo for survival: "Say nothing, trust no one."

I forgot this on a couple of occasions, and ended up in the company of some creep who promised me salvation all wrapped up in ribbons, if I'd only sit on his lonely lap for a while. "Let me show you my magic gizmo," said one.

"That's not magic," I answered, dodging his advances with the help of quick reflexes and sheer dumb luck. Turning out of the alley, I felt completely numb, as I made my way back to nowhere with the determination that somewhere, surely, couldn't be far off.

## hollywood and vine

I always looked forward to our weekly visits to the musicians' union on Vine Street. Dad would go in to check for possible work and take a minute to flirt with Agnes at the front desk, who hounded him because his dues were always in arrears. They had a recreation room there with a pool table and a television where I'd go to watch the guys shoot eight ball, though with all the smoke, it was pretty hard to see.

After these visits, we'd head north to the late, great corner of Hollywood and Vine. I thought it was tops, even as late as '68, '69. There was the Big Owl drugstore on the southeast corner where I'd shoplift, and the Broadway Department Store on the southwest, where I'd do likewise. There was the Firefly, where my dad and Charlie Parker had played—though perhaps not together—and the Brown Derby with the fancy Bamboo Room next door, where I went once for my birthday. Best of all was the On Tray Cafeteria, the best cafeteria, in my opinion, ever. Every time we walked in, Billy Barty, the "little actor with the big career," would be holding court at one of the tables. Somehow my dad knew him. He would wave us over, always with a cigar in his mouth, and have me sit in his lap. Billy was less than four feet tall. It's a little strange, sitting in a midget's lap, but I adored him. He was very animated, as was his circle of colorful friends—guys with names like Lefty, an ex-middleweight southpaw, and Jocko, an alcoholic jockey. I would sit eating my neon Jell-O in sheer heaven, listening to their stories. It was better than Damon Runyon.

My dad, being very funny, a big boxing fan, and an old movie buff, fit in nicely with everyone. Billy called him "Jersey Joe." All of these places are gone now, but back then, the four corners of Hollywood and Vine held some of my brightest memories.

## meeting the chairman

In the summer of '68, Dad and I took a Greyhound bus down to Palm Springs, where he was booked on a two-week gig with a singer named Jimmy Valentino at some mob nightclub. Jimmy was sort of a Vic Damone knockoff, lots of Brylcreem and pinky rings, who smiled too often. What a mismatch they were, but times were lean—Dad took what work he could get. Once in Palm Springs, he hooked up with a local named Dorothy. She was very attractive, a showgirl past her prime but well preserved. Her high baby-blond hairdo was perfectly set and never moved a step out of place. Dorothy's tan was a little well done. She kept her smile tight and controlled so as not to enhance the appearance of laugh lines around her frosty blue eyes.

Dorothy started showing up at every show and coming back to our motel at night. She seemed fairly normal. There was no sign of the weirdness to come. Dad finished fairly early at the club. Palm Springs isn't exactly hopping past a certain hour, and we'd get back in time to see the last half of Johnny Carson and have a pastrami sandwich before bed. One night, Dad stepped outside to fill the ice bucket when he suddenly gasped, jumped back in the room, and locked the door. "Get under the bed," he said to me frantically, waving his arms, which I didn't do. A second later, Dorothy was pounding on the door, screaming things like "You fucking greaseball musician, I'm going to kill you!" Dad and I went to the side window and peeked out to see her stabbing the door with a pair of haircutting scissors, and each time she lunged, her patent leather purse with gold chain strap fell down, and she kept hitching it up, stabbing at the door. I asked my dad what he did to her, why she was mad, but he wouldn't bite— just shrugged. I've wondered, over the years, what would've set her off like that. Maybe he gave her the clap or something.

After fifteen minutes of this, it became apparent that the only thing she was going to hurt was her scissors. We looked at each other and started laughing until we cried, jumping on the bed with my dad doing an evil imperson-ation of poor old Dorothy out there. It was very surreal. The best part came two nights later, when Jimmy Valen-tino showed up at the club with Dorothy on his arm. Dad pulled him aside and said, "Good luck, paisan," and left it at that. Jimmy and Dad didn't get along too well.

Aside from the crazy dame incident, the only other high-light in the desert was meeting Frank Sinatra. He came into the club one night, listened to the music for a couple of hours, then waved my dad over during his break. They had an animated chat about New Jersey, their mothers, baseball, just a couple of nice Italian boys. He bought me a Shirley Temple, shook my dad's hand, told him, "You've got a great book, kid," put a hundred dollars in the tip kitty, and left. I've been down to Palm Springs a few times since

then without my dad, but didn't like it too much. Any-
where I went with him sparkled like a fun fair.

## jump the bum

There was one other kid at the St. Francis, named LaPrez.
He was a nine-year-old mulatto who had a glorious auburn
afro and wild green eyes. I was now seven, very pale and
suspicious.

Being ingenious street kids, we made up games using
what few resources were available to us. Our favorite game
was called "Jump the Bum." Simply put, you would jump
over a street bum until he got pissed off enough to make
a grab for you or, if he really had some moxie, get up and
chase you away. On a bad day, you'd get "dead bums"—too
tired or loaded to budge no matter how much you provoked
them. One time, LaPrez was midleap over our latest victim
when, out of nowhere, the bum pulls out a broken bottle
and slashes open LaPrez's ankle. It took twenty stitches
and kept him out of commission for the rest of the summer. On reflection, perhaps it was a cruel game, but most of
the bums were good sports, almost looking forward to the
attention. It wasn't like any of us had anything better to do.

LaPrez lived with his mother, a very pretty but badly
strung-out hooker. Under the circumstances, I always
thought he was a well-adjusted kid—always able to laugh,
whereas I was eternally sullen. One night, LaPrez came to

our room and asked Dad if he could give him some help with his mother. When he opened the door to their room, she was sitting straight up on a Murphy bed, eyes wide and staring at us, scarf still tied around her arm. She was blue, dead at least an hour.

In the hotel lobby, there was a TV set that three of the resident rummies had total control over, twenty-four hours a day. Usually horse races were on, but for this one fucked-up night, they sat us down on their smelly old-man sofa and let us watch cartoons. LaPrez stared, serious and silent, at the television, and I stared at him. He was staring at Top Cat when the coroners wheeled out his mother, and he did not look up when the police came, inquiring about next of kin (none). Nor did he move when my dad, crying, handed them a bag of his belongings. Then, the cops walked over to him and said something ridiculous like "Come with us, son." It was then that he turned and looked at me, expectant and drowning, and I did nothing. I could have taken his hand or, even better, told him to run. Maybe we both should have run, but my father was sick and needed me—I could never desert him. After that, I was the only kid at the St. Francis. I was like Eloise without the frills.

## feverish

When Mom took off, the one item she left me was her copy of *Flowers of Evil*. "Love, Mom" was inscribed beneath one of the book's woodcuts, each woodcut depicting some agonized individual with head held in hands. I didn't even pick it up for a couple of years, and when I did, my comprehension was minimal. However, I did sense a disturbing connection with the prostitutes and vampires that Baudelaire wrote of. One line that struck a chord in me was "Angel teeming with healthfulness, do you know fever?"

Fever and I were fast friends, courtesy of my chronic asthma. Dr. Byrne often spoke in heavy tones to Dad or Gram, warning them of "possible brain damage," so prolonged were my fevers. Though it is likely that brain cells were sacrificed during the perpetual illness of my youth, it wasn't all in vain. A sustained high fever can produce some wild and vivid fantasies. The fiery mirages I experienced were a welcome respite from reality. On one windy night, as I sat in bed watching the shadows of leaves knocking against the window, each leaf began to morph into a miniature witch on a broomstick. These witches proceeded to fly into the room and perform aerial acrobatics, three feet in front of me. After some time, they lined up and flew out as suddenly as they'd arrived. The leaves of the rubber tree turned back into leaves, and so ended the evening's entertainment. These hallucinations often involved parts of my body. My toes frequently developed faces, each one different and argumentative with each other. The toe people would inquire about my health, ask me to sing a song, wonder how I liked being out of school. "Very much," was always my reply. When I attempted to read during a spiking fever, the book's characters would often appear before me and begin acting out the story as it unfolded. It was like having two sets of eyes. I could at once read and direct my attention to the scenarios being played out before me. I had to be careful what I read. *The Arabian Nights* turned into claustrophobic chaos. I was forced to close the book, only to find that the characters remained, frozen on their horses with swords drawn, wondering what to do next. I pulled the pillows over my head and waited for the fever to break.

I shared these experiences with my father, who had the fearless and fragile heart of a child. "That's wild—fantastic!" he'd enthuse, as I related my latest adventure. The depth of his sincerity always broke my heart.

## corpses

My grandfather died on September 20, 1969. An open-casket service was held at San Fernando Mission. I was there with Dad and Gram, who had her hands full attempting to comfort Grandpop's second wife, Virginia. He had remarried soon after Gram divorced him. I don't remember a lot about Virginia. At the funeral Dad looked thoroughly distraught, which I could never comprehend. This was the man who'd killed and cooked my dad's pet rabbit, then tried to make him eat it. I guess sorrow is a knee-jerk reaction: perhaps we're crying for what might have been. Dad ushered me over to the waxy corpse and said: "Kiss your grandpop goodbye, honey." There was no chance of that, and I visibly squirmed and backed away, looking to Gram for support. "It's the living you should fear, not the dead," she offered. Didn't I know it. Dad let it go and gave Grandpop an extra peck on the forehead for me. Even in death, I could feel his tyranny at work in the small room. It seemed to inspire fear in my father.

It was a great relief to me when our "final goodbyes" were at last over, and I could escape from the too-bright room. Though I'd seen LaPrez's mother's body only a month earlier, it hadn't made me feel uneasy like this. Only sad. The sadness of her life carried over to her death. Dad said her soul would fly straight to the bosom of the Virgin Mary. Grandpop, however, was an odds-on favorite to end up in the big boiler room below. Eternal damnation is the stuff of nightmares, and I had plenty of Poe-style nightmares after that day.

## the haunted elevator

At night, the hallways of the St. Francis were transformed into foreboding corridors fraught with dangers both real and imagined. At the end of the hall there was a window, and a bare red lightbulb illuminating an exit sign. The few other lights that dotted the walls were inevitably broken or burned out. On our floor, there was a perpetually flickering bulb that created an eerie strobe effect, making the images that crept into my peripheral sight twice as disturbing. You could sense that after dark, anything was fair game. Lawlessness prevailed in the hotel, and you could feel it, an agitated air that seemed to wait outside the door. The best bet was to stay put in the room with every light on, the stereo and TV going, and perhaps even a book to complete your distraction.

I couldn't stand the sound of the old elevator, which would stop and open randomly at different floors all night, usually without any passengers. Often when I was on it, it stopped between floors, opening up onto a concrete wall. Ralph, resident bookie and one-eyed ex-jeweler, told me it was haunted. In Ralph's previous life in Vegas, he'd been a jeweler to the mob. Engagement and pinky rings, christening bracelets, brooches for Mama—Ralph was the mob's choice in Las Vegas. Occasionally, he was called on to unload stolen goods, melting down gold and platinum, recutting gems when necessary. One day Ralph was accused of double-crossing a big-time boss, a story he never denied. The boss sent a couple of goons around to cut his right eye for punishment. His right eye was the tool he relied on the most, whether checking the quality of a piece through his magnifier or doing intricate engraving. His eye couldn't be saved. He had it removed and replaced with a glass one that the doctor, a back-alley quack, put in backward. All you could see was the white, while the colored iris apparently rolled around in the back of his head somewhere. Dad had asked why he didn't have it corrected. "Surely they can pop it out and flip it around." Ralph shook his head: "Joe, it's my cross to bear. Besides, it's my inner eye—keeps tabs on my soul."

After being washed up as a jeweler, Ralph moved out to L.A., where he made a living betting on the horses, a full-time job that always kept him busy. He'd track a horse's whole history sometimes, its sire and mare, breeder, trainer. He also had an elaborate theory regarding a jockey's compatibility with a particular horse that at seven years old I didn't really understand. We'd sit in the lobby, a racing form between us, and he'd do his best to school me in the science of betting.

The haunted elevator was one of Ralph's many convictions. He claimed that one night, a former resident who was "real bad news" got on the elevator drunk and pressed two buttons simultaneously, ending up on a floor that exists somewhere between two and three, where likewise dubious characters were destined to dwell for eternity. If that were the case, I thought, three-quarters of the hotel would have been banished long ago to floor 2½, where I imagined carpets of an undistinguishable, depressing color that stank of century-old Thunderbird, with *Welcome to Hell* spelled out in cigarette burns. I knew it was bull, but I opted for the stairs after that, being naturally nervous. It was only three stories, but on a bad day, when the smog hung thick, it was a walk rough on my asthma, and I had to stop several times. My preferred option was to stay inside, where no stairs, haunted elevators, or evil fourth dimensions need concern me.

# kitty

One day, I was on my own in our room, 312, awaiting the return of the television, which Dad was picking up from Harry's pawnshop. They were happy occasions, those days when the TV came out of hock, and I was attempting to make a celebratory "hot plate omelette" when a ferocious banging at the door made me stop cold, filled with dread. I felt certain it was trouble calling, and as I tiptoed over to the door to bolt the latch—which I had opened so I could run down the hallway a dozen times, my daily exercise therapy—I saw the knob turn slowly. Quick as a flash, I was out the window, moving down the fire escape. I was crouching on a second-story landing when a venetian blind was pulled up with a loud, rusty squeal that nearly cost me my footing, especially when I saw the woman standing on the other side of the blind. "What the hell?" she croaked, and pulled me into her room. I'm not sure how old she was, maybe early forties. When you're seven, anyone between the ages of thirty and sixty looks like one universal age somewhere around forty, and that means they're ready to bury. She had big red teased hair, a couple of chins, frosted pink lips and nails, nicotine fingers, and minimal clothes over maximum flesh. Certainly she'd been through the wringer, but a flame still burned in her dark-ringed eyes. She was Kitty Goldstein, and she worked at the Pussycat Theatre on Hollywood Boulevard. "You're the kid upstairs with the nice-looking father. What are you doing lurking out there? You could get hurt." I told her about the stranger at the door, then remembered the hot plate omelette that had probably burned down half the St. Francis by now. Kitty grabbed a kitchen knife and charged up the stairs, an avenging ex-stripper—enough to scare the crap out of anyone.

She burst through our door to find my puzzled father bending over the television, trying to reattach the rabbit ears. "Who the hell are you?" he asked.

"You've got fucking nerve leaving a kid alone," she squawked, and he glanced at me, looking betrayed, while I blurted out my story of a faceless intruder and then noticed that the lousy hot plate must have shorted out, because the eggs were half raw but the switch was still in the on position.

So started a brief union between Dad and Kitty, full of brawling, mad jealousy, and little else. "Get me a piano if you want to make me happy. I can park it right on that roomy ass of yours," coaxed my charming father. Women always complicated our life, but they never lasted long. Kitty became last year's news within five months. To her credit, she'd watch me from time to time and could cook decently when she tried. But she was a boozer, and when she got tight, she got nasty. One day when Kitty had finished a fifth of bourbon, she turned on me and said, "I know what you're thinking—what happened to her? Sure, I suckled at my mother's breast, and Daddy dear bounced me on his knee, so what?" Well, I hadn't been thinking that at all, but I wondered about it plenty after that day. When is the moment people give up, and when do others decide to turn away and cut them out?

## dracula and the man

To eat Chinese takeout on a pulled-out sofa bed, watching *Dracula's Daughter* on the late show, reading magnificent fortune cookie poetry—"Due to your melodic nature, moonlight never misses an appointment"—chain secured on the door, and Dad by my side: surely heaven was a pale place, strictly old hat, when compared with this bliss.

Then the Man would come to the door with his quiet, dead-end knock, poised to piss all over paradise, and I'd look up to check that the dead bolt was bolted. A quick sideways glance at Dad told who would be victorious that evening. I'd tell him, "A vampire can only enter a house if you invite him in." He'd smile and wrap me in his long arms, whispering·that we would not invite the vampire in, and so for this night, his soul would stay intact. Most of the time, my seven-year-old brain could think of nothing clever to say, and the door would be opened. After a short exchange in hushed tones, the inevitable trip to the bathroom. When Dad emerged, it was not the same, and I'd hastily feign sleep and wish I had a stake to drive through the Man's heart, if he had one. At times, I could see that Dad needed the Man, and we'd go looking for him, though I was told only that we were getting fresh air or buying milk. We'd make our way to the liquor store a few doors down and always stand at the same telephone booth, Dad shifting nervously, pretending to make a call that mysteriously never connected.

One night, I saw the Man first and did not tell, then fell into ten-ton guilt, because Dad got sick, and two bottles of cough syrup did little to help. I'd struggle with right and wrong and come to no conclusions. Usually, the Man would find him, and I would avoid his eyes for fear of falling under an evil spell. "Aren't you a pretty thing," he'd say like whispering death, brushing my cheek with two soft, cold fingers that would stay forever on my face.

## the cake bride

Fazzi's, which stood on Western Avenue between Hollywood and Sunset, was a mecca for Italian groceries. To walk through its doors was to enter someplace holy. When we had the occasion to treat ourselves, Dad and I would head over and carefully select our favorite items. A half-pint box of Sicilian olives and a hard roll were all that I desired. Dad went for the prosciutto and capicola, and the mortadella that melted in your mouth if they sliced it thin enough. The albacore tuna packed in good olive oil was fine right out the can.

Fazzi's had a basket full of two-foot-long bacala. Dad would grab one and challenge me to a duel. "Step down, in the name of good King Richard!" he'd shout, backing me into a case of tomato paste with the smelly dried fish pointed at my nose. A dirty look and a stern *"Che fai?"* from the owner usually put an end to our game.

Across the street from the market was Fazzi's Bakery. The smell in there made me swoon. It was almost impossible to describe: warm sugar, almond paste, rum extract, and unknown sublime odors that swirled together, blessing a half-block radius with an ethereal aroma. In the window stood a giant multitiered wedding cake. It was covered with the palest pink frosting, trimmed with some lacelike confection and little white plastic lilies. The perfect porcelain bride and groom were perched on top. The base of the cake was surrounded by small net bags filled with silver- and gold-coated almonds, the kind they give out at Italian weddings. It took my breath away. Marie the mustached lady always gave me an amaretto cookie, which I'd promptly hide until I found a secure area where I could enjoy it without the fear of being seen. Sometimes I'd save half for Dad, who had a terrible sweet tooth, even without dope. He'd make some coffee, dunk his cookie, and roll his eyes, making ecstatic eating sounds that made me laugh.

I invented a game in which I imagined that I was the porcelain bride on the wedding cake. I would stand perfectly poised and silent in my one ragged party dress, up on a chair or table, and pretend that I was untouchable. It used to make Dad nervous. "Hey—what do you call that game? Are you a zombie queen or what?" I would never answer him. I remained inanimate and serene, existing atop my sugary oasis for as long as my mortal legs could stand it.

# probation

Dad had a series of probation officers he had to check in with regularly. The one I remember most clearly was a man by the absurd name of Mr. Wumplebottom. Dad reported to his PO every couple of weeks, informing him of upcoming work and assuring him that he was staying clean. He really sweated it. On those days, we took the bus down to Wilshire Boulevard for the "third degree," as Dad referred to it. Personally, I looked forward to his interviews, because we'd usually go to a nearby movie theater afterward. I saw *Easy Rider*, *Butch Cassidy and the Sundance Kid*, *Midnight Cowboy*, and a few other films that didn't make quite as strong an impression. I'm eternally grateful that Dad didn't concern himself with which movies were age appropriate for a seven-year-old. The only criterion was that they were good, and back then, they were.

One day Dad's usual anxiety was particularly bad. I felt I could see it crushing him under its weight. When we entered Wumplebottom's office, Dad sat nervously, looking down between long, fidgeting legs, tight mouthed, clasping and unclasping his hands. Wumplebottom let him suffer a while before speaking. "I received some information that has been verified." Long pause. "You violated your parole."

"That bitch," Dad muttered.

"Ah, *cherchez la femme*, ha ha. Whatever the case may be, I'm now left with the unpleasant task of what to do, what to do." Wumplebottom's sigh was a death rattle void of all empathy. He enjoyed his work, all right. Poor Dad. This was the second time that I knew of when an angry female had turned canary on him, prompted usually by some real or imagined infidelity. Wumplebottom now turned his reptilian eyes on me and, holding out a too-pretty hand, beckoned me over. I looked at Dad, who was still averting his eyes, and decided it was best to comply. Wumplebottom lifted me onto his knee, patting my leg, and continued. "Joe, I could have you turned over, right now, have your sweet child here placed in protective custody." I felt like I'd just been pushed off a cliff. I was free-falling and unable to speak. Now I looked desperately to Dad, who was intently gazing at last year's gum on the floor. "I don't enjoy this. I'm here to help, if you'll work with me." Suddenly and casually, he lifted my dress, asking: "Does Daddy take good care of you?" Dad looked up then, for a split second, and next I knew, I was waiting outside the office with the receptionist giving me pitiful looks, expecting the police to bust through the door at any time.

Bad guys, it seemed, were everywhere. The only difference was how up front they were about it. As I sat waiting, I recalled that the sun had been shining in Dad's face. I knew it was so, because it had reflected off his steely curls when his head was hanging down. He hadn't even seen where Wumplebottom had his hands. I felt vaguely relieved. After that day, all office visits ceased. I went to Gram's for a short time, and Dad disappeared, saying simply, "I have to cool it for a while, okay?"

"Why ask me?" I thought. Kids have no say in their lives. When we were reunited, Dad never spoke of that day. Things were soon back to normal, whatever normal was within the twisted walls of our life.

## is that all there is?

As a child, I tried to adhere to the same simple philosophy that many children have. I did my best to find love in some form, even when it appeared to be absent, and I tried to seek out beauty, though it wasn't often present in any traditional sense. I found that it was always best to keep my thoughts private and attempted to avoid situations that had a potential for conflict. This last credo would prove particularly challenging. It was never wise to provoke or even engage in conversation with my dad after he had fixed. If you left him alone and buried your nose in a book, he would weather his high with only a few random outbursts that he usually directed at himself. Often his ranting would manifest itself in the form of a one-sided battle with an invisible foe I always assumed was the Devil. "You're not God—I know who you are," he'd yell, pointing at the air before him. My book would begin to slip out of my hands from the amount of sweat I'd shed over the possibility that Satan was in the room with us.

He'd then go over to the piano and bang out some dissonant chords repeatedly, stopping at times to tell me how much he loved me or how much he hated the cold fucking world. Unfortunately, when we both lived with my grand-mother, as we occasionally did, she was not able to ignore these drug interludes. Dad would emerge from the bed-room with a dull and distant, totally unfamiliar expression. As much as I warned her against it, Gram felt compelled to start in on him, tsk-tsking with her dark, agonized eyes and sad gray head. "Look at yourself. My God, my God." I'd tug furiously on her sleeve, beseeching her silence.

"Fuck your God, and fuck you," he'd slur, his mouth set in an ugly scowl. Things would escalate rapidly, and he'd say stuff that I understood to be totally contrary to his true nature. When straight, he was the quintessential loving, worshipful Italian son.

One night, Gram went for a full frontal assault. Dad had been peeling an apple and was still holding the knife. "Why don't you just kill me?" she wailed at him, beating her chest.

"Maybe I should," Dad answered, taking two steps to-ward her, waving the knife. That was it. I jumped in front of Gram, horrified, and prepared to die. "You stay away from her—I hate you!"

Gram grabbed my arm and swung me around to face her. "Amy, don't you dare speak to your father that way!" What was *this*? I thought, totally mystified. I looked back and forth between the two of them, and they looked at me as though I'd had an inappropriate fit in the middle of a church picnic.

Some kids would be much better off without the added confusion of an adult point of view. It destroys the purity of their world. Perhaps Gram and Dad found some bizarre contentment in these exchanges. I walked into the bedroom and put Peggy Lee's "Is That All There Is?" on the record player.

## the bakers

For a short period of time, Dad assigned us a new surname. For half of 1969, we became Amy and Joe Baker. From what I could piece together, he'd given the name of a local drug dealer to the authorities to avoid jail time and feared reprisals.

My father would've gone to any lengths to avoid prison. At the age of twenty, he was arrested on drug charges and sent to Riker's Prison. On the day he began serving sentence, he was given what's known as a "blanket job." Seven men got him alone in the corridor, threw a blanket over his head, and proceeded to sexually assault him. He spent five days in the prison's hospital ward, only to be released into the same situation. Apparently, this is America's remedy for reforming young addicts. Having survived this ordeal, and frequently reliving it in his mind, he found the idea of being locked up particularly unbearable. Had I been in his shoes, I'd have ratted out the Christ child and many others to avoid jail time. However, since he was a decent and loyal guy at heart, his singing only added a new demon to his host of others. We would be sitting having a meal when suddenly he'd freeze, a forkful of food halfway to his mouth, and say: "What are you looking at? I'm not a fink."

I'd do my best to ignore these outbursts. I knew they were connected to the fact that I now had to write "Amy Baker" on all my school papers. Though supposedly hiding, we never moved apartments or switched hair colors. Only the last name changed. All this led to my first serious bout of paranoia. I took to looking over my shoulder while walking, waiting to be abducted, at the very least, by some angry, faceless con. After five months or so, word came that the drug dealer in question had come to a nasty end, courtesy of a shiv in the stomach. Though pleased to be an Albany again, I never got over an intense feeling of unease that lives ever vigilant on the back of my neck.

## no brakes

It was the tail end of summer, late one afternoon, when I found myself in the back of a brand-new Dodge Dart convertible. Dad was next to me, his friend Vinnie drove, and the great Terry Southern was the front-seat passenger. The Stones' "Satisfaction" was on the radio, and Dad, possessed by Terpischore, the muse of dance, stood up and danced in the backseat as we flew around some hilly part of East L.A. They were all high and whooping it, getting big kicks out of small things. Vinnie suddenly announced, "Shit, the brakes are out!" I started to notice that we were sailing along at an accelerated speed, and Vinnie was whiter than usual, but Dad and Mr. Southern only laughed. I decided that their laughter would cheat death, and though nervous, I felt exhilarated. Now we were getting air when we came off the hills, and hell if Dad wasn't still standing there hoofing it, snapping his fingers and rolling his shoulders, a cigarette dangling between serenely smiling lips. After we ran a couple of red lights, with Vinnie laying on the horn, Mr. Southern started reciting, "Though I walk through the valley of the shadow of death . . ." Dad reached forward and pulled hard on the hand brake to the right of Vinnie's knee. The smell of burning tires was intense as we came to a halt at the top of the sidewalk, just grazing a bus bench. Dad's upper body was in the front seat, his long legs in the air, while Vinnie sat with his head against the wheel and Mr. Southern said, "Joe get those boats out of my face." My heart was pounding madly, my mind wild with images of being mangled, when these thoughts were suddenly banished by their laughter and the steady defiance of the Stones, still playing on the radio. Dad righted himself and grabbed me reassuringly. "You okay, baby? That was exciting, wasn't it?"

Vinnie was bugged because he'd scraped some paint off the right side of his brother's new car, but other than that, no one was hurt, and thankfully, the police didn't show. Mr. Southern said something about being lucky, and maybe they should "go bet on the ponies." A call was made, and after a while Vinnie's girl showed up and I was dropped off at Gram's. The three of them went off in search of a new adventure with their female chauffeur in tow.

As I sat with my head on my grandmother's lap, breathing in the strong warmth that always surrounded her, I had a sad epiphany: I wanted to be a guy. Women could shout from podiums, rack up college degrees, burn their bras, and build their muscles, but they'd never possess "it." "It" being man's capacity for a certain swaggering joy, a supremely liberated confidence that is rarely deflated by the opinions of others. It's those inborn *coglioni*, or nuts, that come with the knowledge that you are the chosen gender and will always rule the world.

# replay

There is a point where love of music can give way to unhealthy obsession. I would (and still can) listen to the same song one hundred, two hundred times in a row easily—not necessarily the whole song, sometimes just the introduction, a solo, the bridge, et cetera. My hand would hover nervously over the record needle, or fingers tapping on the rewind button, desperate to hear it again and again. This habit was not driven by pleasure as much as obsession. It was a necessity that the song not end. As long as it continued, I was somehow safe from all enemies, both real and imagined, whoever they were at the time. I've spent nine or ten hours at a stretch doing this. At the age of eight, there

were a few days when I decided the key to my salvation
lay in the bridge of "You Do Something to Me" as sung by
Marlene Dietrich.

On one particular day, Dad was having an ugly fight
with a girlfriend, Jackie, over matters of dope and sex so
lurid that I felt my head would explode if I heard another
word. I turned up the stereo to its maximum capacity and
pressed my forehead into the tattered speaker grille. With
eyes closed, one hand poised atop the record arm, I listened
to the soothing voice of Dietrich, pouring lazy as honey
over the beauty of Cole Porter. I was just beginning to feel
at ease when Jackie rushed over, snatched the record away,
and sent it sailing out the window. Something so sacred
hurled to its death like a cheap Frisbee. I guess it felt simi-
lar to someone punching you full force when you're deep in
the middle of a favorite dream. "*What* is wrong with your
fucking kid? She's as crazy as you are!" I drank in the calm
air of divine justice, for I knew Jackie had just stepped over
the line. Dad lunged at her with assured grace and grabbed
her blue-black hair like an Apache dancer, dragging her
through the door, down the hall, and out of our lives. I was
sitting with my hands over my ears and my head in my
knees when Dad lifted me in his arms and began to sing:
"Let me live 'neath your spell, do do that voodoo that you
do so well . . ." Over and over he sang, and I quietly rejoiced
that we were both as mad as each other.

# i, spartacus

Dad signed up for the methadone program in January 1970, and a visit to the clinic became part of his daily routine. On the weekends, when I didn't have school, I'd travel with him from Gram's, where we were once again living, to a clinic in the San Fernando Valley that seemed a hundred miles away. It appeared that people were sent to the farthest, most inconvenient place possible—perhaps the system's way of saying: "We know you're desperate for your dose, and we're going to bust your chops about it just because we can." One married couple Dad knew, Mary and Joe, had to bus all the way out to Pomona from Hollywood for their methadone. A month into this daily nightmare on the not-so-rapid transit system, Mary became very ill and was admitted to UCLA Medical Center with some rare form of lupus. Her husband, Joe, then had to travel from Hollywood, to Pomona, to the hospital in Westwood. After a week or so, he was chipping in order to cut down on the Pomona trips, but was soon found out and terminated from the program. Joe started borrowing a car from a sympathetic neighbor to make the ride to visit Mary, which worked out well until the day he crashed while driving loaded and was brought in DOA to the same hospital as his wife. She didn't last too long after that, and it was just as well. The medical center was getting ready to kick her out anyway, for nonpayment of bills.

One overcast Sunday found Dad in an exceptionally joyful, mischievous mood as we hung around the clinic waiting room. The night before, we'd watched *Spartacus*, one of his favorite movies, on the late show. When you needed to escape life's rough edges for a few hours, nothing could beat seeing a great film. Most everyone around us looked understandably miserable. If this was how they spent Saturday, chances were their lives were none too bright and breezy. Dad recognized a couple of the guys there, not surprisingly both musicians, and they embarked on a loud and boisterous conversation about film music scores. The exasperated-looking woman behind the reception desk slid back the glass divider and, glaring at Dad, yelled, "Hey! Pipe down, you, you—what *is* your name?" Dad looked at her with mock surprise, then jumped up on his chair, shouting, "I am Spartacus!"—at which both of his acquaintances and, incredibly, two complete strangers followed suit. There were a total of five madmen standing tall on fiberglass chairs, beating their chests or hands on hips, yelling "I am—Spartacus!" Dad looked down at me and winked, smiling with his pearly Clark Gable dentures, and I thought he was the world's biggest star, far too big for the galaxy to contain. The gruff receptionist, not overly impressed by this scene, and probably accustomed to bizarre behavior, shook her head, saying, "You is all crazy, that's what you is." She slammed the divider closed and went back to her magazine. A buzz that felt like hope ran through the place, and now almost everyone, except for those too sick, was laughing. It was the power of cinema in action. A movie could turn a meth clinic into a great coliseum, where all the junkies were transformed into mighty gladiators, even if only for one wild moment.

## valentine

In January 1970, Dad and I moved into a little studio apartment on Gramercy Place. Things seemed to be looking up until Dad got busted on Valentine's Day for some probation violation.

Early on the evening of the fourteenth, I was waiting for him to return from the store. We were planning a Valentine's party for just us two broken-down sweethearts. I was listening to Fats Waller's "Fat and Greasy," which was feeling-good music, as opposed to Billie singing "What's New," which I'd play when I was low. Anyway, I was looking out the window for Dad when I spotted a cop car and an unmarked vehicle with two thinly disguised narcs inside. The uniforms would look up at the window occasionally, but the narcs stared straight ahead. Half an hour they sat, but in our neighborhood, stakeouts were a common sight, so I didn't give it much thought.

Then, up the drive sauntered my father. His walk was most musical and swinging, like all his gestures. He was carrying a bag and looking up at the window, starting to wave, when he spotted the cops and they spotted him. They jumped out, grabbed his hand, still midwave, pulled it down between his legs, pulled his other hand up between his legs, and cuffed him that way—like a contortionist. They were pushing him into the back of the unmarked car just as I got outside. He was looking at me, yelling, "Everything's okay!"—very unconvincing. I looked at the ground at all the little things that had spilled out of his bag. Little candy hearts with sayings like GROOVY, KISS ME, et cetera, hot dogs, a couple of Yoo-Hoo chocolate drinks, and a card. The illustration on the card was classic liquor store art, with a cartoon guy who looked like Mr. Magoo, with a big red nose, striped prison garb, and a ball and chain with hearts around it. It said: "I'm just a prisoner of your love." I reached down for it, but an officer grabbed me from behind. His mistake. I scratched, spit, and punched, trying to get my hands on that card, to no avail. Things become vague after that. I think I had a major asthma attack, as I was inclined to do under duress. At that point in my life, I had seen a few fairly nasty things, but to this day, the thought of that card can cause me more pain, and make me cry more deeply, than all the loss and sorrow in the world. After Dad went down, they decreased his methadone dose from ninety to ten milligrams a day as "punishment." Of course all that did, besides making him sick, was force him to supplement—and he was off again.

## tunnel rats

In 1970, the war in Vietnam was an obvious concern for anyone who was half conscious at the time. I remember reading a harrowing piece in *Life* magazine on the Tunnel Rats of Cu Chi. The Tunnel Rats were American Special Forces who had the undesirable task of lowering themselves into holes they could just squeeze through, trying to secure the labyrinth of black tunnels, two hundred miles' worth, that the Viet Cong were operating out of. The tunnels were often booby-trapped in a variety of horrible, imaginative ways, and the solider going into one had no idea what he'd find as he groped along in the narrow pitch darkness.

I don't know if it was my acute fear of the dark, my perverse interest in war, or both that riveted me to this particular article, but I know it haunted me endlessly. I cut it out and pasted it into my scrapbook entitled *Bad Rotten Stuff*. This article was a prime example of "things could be worse" for me. I could be a Tunnel Rat. When something screwed up occurred that couldn't be placated by the sweetness of some old, conjured lyric or by thoughts of Jerry Lewis, I would turn 180 degrees in the opposite direction. A look at *Bad Rotten Stuff* usually shifted my desperate perspective. Strange sometimes, the incidents that send you over the edge when you're young.

Dad spent some time in the company of a girl named Ronda. I couldn't say exactly, but I'd guess she was twenty or so, compared to Dad's forty-six years. Perhaps forty-six is about the age when men begin to sense their mortality, and fear sets in regarding their waning appeal to the fairer sex. I don't know.

I do know that there was no outwardly obvious reason for Dad to take up with this girl. She wasn't his type at all. She looked like a Manson follower—hairy and frumpy. Spaced out. Up to this point, I'd had a lot of exposure to the drug culture but not much exposure to sex. I wasn't sure what people got up to in that arena, and I didn't much care to find out.

One night, I was rudely awakened by the sound of Ronda yelling at my dad. They were holed up in the bathroom, the fate of all his encounters, since I slept in the only room, and he was thankfully discreet in these matters. "Deeper, harder." Ronda was barking orders at Dad like a brigadier general. Though I had some vague notion of what was afoot, it sounded so severe I barely resisted running interference on my dad's behalf. It was clear she wasn't going to shut up anytime soon. I tried burying my head inside of the couch bed, but she was a bigmouth. I started to feel inexplicably sick from it and turned my thoughts to the poor, unsuspecting Tunnel Rats and the various fates that awaited them. "Now. Do it now!" she continued. There were vipers hidden in bamboo, rigged so a solider could unwittingly tip the deadly snake out, and onto his neck or face, if he hit the bamboo with his helmet. "Give it to me harder!" Spears were mounted below that would run through their groins as they descended. "Deeper, deeper." Baskets of scorpions were released from the ceiling when they stepped on a tripwire.

It was no use. My head was imploding. Just as I was removing myself out to the fire escape to get some sleep, I heard Dad speak. It was a comfort knowing he hadn't

been beaten into a coma. "Ah, why don't you SHUT UP?"
he yelled. Lovely silence. Next day, Dad looked haggard
and somewhat disheartened. "I think she's gross," I volun-
teered in an attempt to cheer him up. He chuckled weakly,
nudging me on the head. "Yeah, well, she's pretty young." I
hoped that I wouldn't have to explore the dark, mysterious
tunnels of sex for many years to come.

## lyrics

One night while sitting on the sofa bed watching *Top Hat*
on Movies Till Dawn, Dad grabbed my hand, saying, "Listen, listen to this." The song was "Cheek to Cheek," and
the line that caused his rapture was "The cares that hung
around me through the week, seem to vanish like a gam-
bler's lucky streak." Dad sang this as if Irving Berlin had
given him the key to squaring his sins with God and the
Devil. "The existence of songs like that give one hope in
this lousy world," he exclaimed.

This remark was a revelation to me. The next day, I began writing parts of lyrics that in some way inspired hope
in me, until I had filled up both sides of a sheet of notebook
paper, which I folded carefully and carried with me everywhere. In moments of upheaval, spiritual or otherwise, I'd
take it out and read these words like sacred scriptures.

*School* was the ugliest word I knew. I had a knack for at-
tracting abuse from students and teachers alike. Perhaps my

appearance was off-putting; I was oblivious to the fashions of 1970 and favored some bright yellow shoes and a red vinyl raincoat that I wore regardless of the weather. When no women were in my life to tend to my hair, it resembled a large, deserted nest, and my incessant wheezing didn't help my case much either. I'd pull out my lyrics often during class, which roused the curiosity of future cheerleader Susie Wheeler, who sat to my right. "What's that? A letter from your boyfriend, Stinky Sid?" Stinky Sid was my male equivalent: a shy, skinny, friendless nose picker who was also obsessed with horror movies. I tried to ignore Susie's taunts, but she wouldn't have it. She grabbed my paper and began reading it aloud as I chased her around desks and felt my chest turn to brick. For a moron, she was surprisingly adept at running and reading at the same time.

"'I'd tear the stars down from the sky for you.' Hey! This *is* a love letter! 'You're the purple light of a summer night in Spain.' You are such a freak!" she wailed. "'Where troubles melt like lemon drops—'" She ran to the window to throw the paper out, and as she leaned over, I crashed the window down across her back, holding it fast. I thrilled to hear her laughter turn to screams. Our ineffectual teacher, Mrs. Stern, finally intervened, grabbing my hair in an attempt to pull me away. However, hate and adrenaline made me strong, and I would not be moved, not until Stinky Sid looked at me as if to say, "It's no use—not for the likes of us." Only then did I loosen my grip. Susie's parents filed a complaint and called my father, who told them flatly that they were a family of square turds. Glorious suspension followed, and for one week, I read—and listened to—all the lovely lyrics I desired, without fear of interruption.

## terry

Terry loved Dad. She cooked for him, occasionally copped for him—and was a big jazz fan. When he was abusive, she cried silent, dignified tears. Her appearance was striking. Waist-length honey hair, neatly pressed minis, matching bags and shoes.

Terry was a transvestite. She would say (I must say *she*, never having seen her as a he) that if real women spent half the time that she did "enhancing their femininity," the world would be full of happy men. Terry was forever saving money for her sex-change operation, and Dad was forever blowing her savings on smack. To further complicate her life, she got saddled with the responsibility of caring for me. Terry often read me fairy tales. It was a treat to hear "Little Red Riding Hood" read by someone whose natural baritone made as convincing a wolf as her cultivated high voice did a Red Riding Hood.

By mid-1970, my asthma had spiraled out of control. I spent a large amount of time at the Children's Hospital ER on Vermont Avenue waiting for adrenaline shots that brought only short-lived relief. The doctors seemed at a loss to offer any sound advice concerning my condition and would suggest odd things like "Drink a lot of Bubble-Up" or "Try breathing like a fish," whatever the hell that meant. My world was a steaming inferno of vaporizers, and I was constantly slathered in Vick's.

Dad decided that a couple of days away from the L.A. smog would help free my laboring lungs, and so a road trip ensued: Dad, his friend Vince, who was the only person we knew who hadn't had his driver's license revoked, and Terry. Though this time it was not the great Terry Southern but our new Terry in the car. We headed up the 610 to Arrowhead in a '66 gray-primered Fairlane. Vince was the poster boy for junkies everywhere, with skin like school paste, sunken black eyes, and concave cheeks. He would've had better luck frightening predators away with a single glance than with the small pearl-handled revolver he brought along for protection. "Vince, you mook, that's a chick's gun," Dad laughed.

Dad packed for this outing like he would for a weekend gig in Vegas—cuff links, Aqua Velva, shoe shine kit, and a sheet of blotter acid he had procured from some young musician who was playing with the Mothers of Invention and who assured Dad that Arrowhead would be the ideal place to trip for the first time. If there was ever a person born who should have steered clear of LSD, it was my father, who spent much of his life plagued by wild flights of paranoid fancy without the aid of hallucinogens. Terry looked like the Swiss Miss cocoa ad come to life in two-dimensional drag, with long hair braided and looped over, and size eleven white mary janes. Always astonishing and impractical, from head to toe.

Upon arrival, we explored just long enough to find a clearing, where we parked ourselves on airline blankets and Dad said, "Isn't this the grooviest?" as we squinted at the sunlit pines, a group of city vampires who would have surely perished in the wild after a very short time. The day seemed endless—I imagined the lake being dragged for bodies and robbers on the lam hiding out in forest cabins. Anything to make it interesting. Boredom eventually prevailed, and I fell asleep around seven, listening to Dad and company preparing to take a second hit of acid, having felt nothing from the first after all of fifteen minutes. Stretched out across the front bench seat of the Ford, I was startled out of sleep by a mad howling. Looking out the windshield, I saw Dad crouched on a boulder baying at the moonless sky, as Terry danced around him, a demented Isadora Duncan, singing in a sweet falsetto. Vince was lying silently on his back. After a while, I too lay down, staring at mysterious stains on the headliner. I decided then that there was nothing terribly relaxing about nature. I couldn't particularly breathe better, and the cafeteria counters at the On Tray or Clifton's were far more attractive than any grouping of trees. At least in the city, my enemies were not so faceless.

Terry proved to be a much better mother than my natural one. She baked cookies, put me in French braids with blue ribbons to match my eyes, and even joined the PTA—June

Cleaver with a dick. Unfortunately, some concerned father had figured out that she was a he, and made the mistake of confronting her after school one day. Now Terry Femme, in her prior incarnation, she had been Terence the Terror, Golden Gloves, and with one left jab to the sternum she set this asshole on his knees. She smoothed out her skirt, gently took my hand, and earned herself a place on my short list of heroines.

However, this scene of twisted domesticity was short-lived. Terry had never had a real habit—just the occasional "joy bang," as they say—but soon she was using in earnest. She was so tormented, one couldn't blame her. Maybe she was testing Dad's devotion, seeing if he'd intervene, she pined over him so. The problem is, junkies are usually self-absorbed. I don't think he noticed her decline—but I did. She started turning tricks, and after being picked up on a second charge of pandering and possession, she cut a deal with the DA to avoid a two-year stretch in a men's prison—her worst fear. After informing on her dealer, she simply disappeared, and I never saw her again.

So began one of life's little slumps. School became simply unbearable. Even in Hollywood, my home life was fodder for gossip. Now I had Dad picking me up stoned at the front of the school. He would wait by the gate, scatting to himself and swaying, grabbing at the invisible fairies that danced above his head. One boy, Dougie, took to impersonating his strung-out state for the class's amusement, including the teacher, who seemed to get the biggest bang out of it. This went on for a few days until I finally snapped. It was a Thursday when I kicked the offensive boy's ass. I bloodied his nose and cut his lip. When they finally pulled me off him, I called my teacher Mrs. Stern an ugly old cunt, and at the tender age of eight, I was expelled from Grant Elementary School.

## mr. tambourine man

My father's firm conviction that I possessed some singing ability can only be chalked up to irrational parental love that rendered him totally deaf. When the time came for the school variety show, it was decided that I would sing a song. "Why don't you do that 'Tambourine' number you always sing along to? You sound like an angel." He beamed reassuringly. "Mr. Tambourine Man," the Byrds' version, was my favorite 45, and I played it constantly and sang along to it like a castrated mouse, not an angel. On the night of the show, I knew I was doomed, even before the rusty relic accompanying me on the piano botched the opening chords. I stood on the auditorium stage looking out at all the kids and their parents and started to drown. I attempted to sing, but hardly any sound came out of my mouth. Someone shouted "louder" while others rolled their eyes, nudging each other, and some kid named Raymond made lewd gestures, sticking his tongue through the V of his fingers, which threw me so much I forgot my place in the song. When it ended, so too ended any further thought of it. I'd had worse ordeals, certainly, so I filed it away, knowing I had tried my best.

Ten years later I'd have more success performing the same song for what appeared to be a Japanese Mafia convention. That time I kept my mouth shut. I danced with nothing more than a pair of tambourines and a see-through poncho covering my only natural talents. It was good money the first few times I did it, but the money, to my thinking, was the only reason to do it. I'd never get that "buzz" from performing that Dad so often spoke of. Getting up in front of a roomful of strangers, whether they liked me or not, would never give me any pleasure. However, had I possessed even half of my dad's talent, I might have had a different song to sing.

# speeding

Certain people are not compatible with certain drugs, in much the same way that one can meet a person and have an immediate affinity or a violent dislike toward them. They say it's chemistry. I'm sure it is, in the case of drugs. I don't know the precise time when Dad got into speed, but I do remember the first time I saw him on it right after he fixed. He and speed were a match made in hell. Maybe he used too much, or he shot something weird, like human adrenaline, but it was the first time I felt truly fearful, along with the usual frustration and sadness.

We were alone in the apartment, and Dad had been acting cagey and distracted, when he left for the bathroom, leaving me to watch *On the Waterfront* on our lousy TV. It had a broken vertical hold, so you watched movies with a constant black vertical band moving up the screen at half-second intervals.

The first thing I noticed was how quickly he emerged from the bathroom, not like his usual rendezvous with heroin, where he'd stay ten minutes or so while he came on, and then, when ready, float onto the couch, keeping one toe in my world. A conscious effort, I felt, not to shut me out completely. On this day, he charged into the room, making a hole in the wall where the knob crashed into it. He paced around madly, sort of hunched, and for a minute, I thought he was doing an impression (which he was great at) of Groucho, one of his favorites. Then I saw the torrents of sweat pouring off him and the veins on his neck and forehead bulging and straining against his flesh. His mouth was pulled tight, teeth clenched hard, like a death's-head. He rubbed his arms and looked at me with wild eyes that tried to communicate but couldn't.

I went into the bathroom and was shocked to see he'd left his works sitting out. This was something he never did. He always stashed them in a black leather bag that he kept under the sink. It chilled me to see it all there on top of the basin like a prop from *I Was a Teenage Werewolf*, which it appeared that Dad was acting out in the other room. Being clueless in these matters, I ran him a hot bath and wished there was some booze in the house. He'd sworn off that two years earlier, when he vomited pints of blood and was rushed to the hospital for transfusions while the doctor shook his head like an undertaker, saying, "He'll probably die."

I'm not sure if the bath helped, or if he'd just passed his peak, but he started to gain some control. His mouth relaxed, and his veins subsided. He looked at me from the tub, shaking and wet. "I'm sorry, baby, I'm sorry." I forced an insincere smile. Poor guy. He'd just had a date with a fast bitch, a raving psychotic, who almost killed him. Best he stuck with his quiet, gentler love, the one who smoothed his brow and lifted his cares. She too might kill him, but heroin appeared to be the more painless path to travel. I returned to my movie just as Terry gave his big speech to Johnny in the back of the car: "You were my little brother, you should have looked out for me, just a little. I could have been somebody, instead of a bum, which I am." Brando was preaching from his pulpit, and I embraced his words with my whole being. It was St. Jude's Church of Hopeless Souls, and I was its eight-year-old, front-row-center convert. I picked at my holey, dirty socks and made a mental note to five-finger some new ones in the morning.

## music lessons

Musical education at the hands of my dad was both exhilarating and, at times, a terrible drag. He expected so much from me, which I'm not knocking, but I was a fairly average eight-year-old, only capable of retaining so much information. Because I was his daughter and tuned into him on other levels, he assumed that I had the same ability that he did to understand jazz. Of course, I had only been listening to music for a quarter of the time he'd been playing it. I was barraged with technical terms and abstract theories. He was very keen on contemporary composers like Schoenberg too, but the whole atonal thing made me weep with confusion, so he laid off of that, and we stuck with jazz.

As much as I like jazz, when I was forced to analyze and recognize every flatted fifth, suspended harmony, and mopmop lick, it would start to grind me down. I was a nervous wreck when we listened to music together, because I knew I'd fail the test to come—usually figuring out the origins of bebop tunes, what popular songs they were derived from. I sucked at that, much to my Dad's dismay. "You mean you can't hear that 'Hot House' is 'What Is This Thing Called Love?' What a tin ear." Oh well, I fared better with the standards—knew most of them after the first couple notes of the verse, but that was memorization, plain and simple. One Father's Day, I bought Dad some Bird anthology and told him I liked the "My Old Flame" track. He let me know that this particular recording was a really poor one. "He's so loaded—can't you hear all the spit in his reed?" Guess not. Anyway, I'm very grateful for those learning sessions, and I'd like to think that if he were still around, he might be half pleased with my efforts to keep learning, and very pleased that the love of music he instilled in me has helped me pull through some rough times.

OCT • 57

CLOCKWISE FROM TOP: Making music with Warne Marsh (sax), Bob Whitlock (bass), and Sam Dembowski (drums), 1957; Right combo: relaxing during the recording of *The Right Combination* in engineer Ralph Garretson's living room, 1957; Into the light after an all-night jam session, around 1945

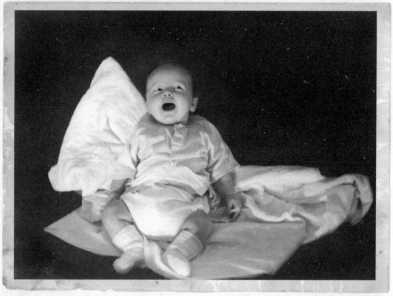

CLOCKWISE FROM TOP LEFT ON THIS PAGE: Mr. and Mrs. Joe Albany, publicity shot, 1960; Mom, poised fragility on a Hollywood Street, 1963; ". . . and that was the beginning of fairies," 1962

OPPOSITE PAGE: (Top) Happiness with tiny Chiclets, 1967. (Bottom right) Portrait, girl out of time, 1974. (Bottom left) Party dress, late '60s

OPPOSITE PAGE: (Top) Inspiration all around, France, mid-'70s; (Bottom) Dad, older but happier for a while, around 1979

THIS PAGE: (Top) Reunited: Dad back at Gram's for a visit from Europe, 1977; (Bottom) Getting down to business, Europe, mid-'70s

# izzy

In 1971, Dad had a couple of friends living at the Knickerbocker Hotel over on Ivar, the most interesting being a guy
named Izzy who made a living doing astrological charts.
Izzy informed my dad that on the fourth, fifth, and sixth of
February in 1962, a mass of people in India ran to the top
of a mountain because the planets were all aligned, which
signaled either the end of the world or the birth of the
new messiah. Since I was born February 5, 1962, Izzy fixed
on the idea that my life should be closely monitored and
insisted that we visit him on a regular basis so he could
see what was new in my chart. He had a studio apartment
on the eighth floor that looked south to Hollywood Boulevard, and four cats that stank up the place—he never
cracked a window, chain-smoked cigars.

Izzy would answer the door in a red Chinese robe but
had the countenance of a kindly bookie. He always played
jazz, knew my dad from Greenwich Village back in '44,
when he'd been a local scenester, respected writer, and
great music supporter. However, times change, and those
who don't get steamrolled into oblivion. That's what happened to Izzy, who'd been living at the Knickerbocker for
sixteen years, since '55. He'd decided to hole himself up
surrounded by his memories and passions. Hotels in Hollywood and downtown L.A. are full of forgotten people
like that. People you wouldn't look twice at, with their
hot plates and old slippers, but you should look, because

they're often far more interesting than all the rich assholes swanning around Beverly Hills, full of themselves and nothing else.

The last time I saw Izzy was late '72. I was with my grandmother at the beauty salon inside the Knickerbocker when I spotted him through the beauty shop window having his shoes shined in the lobby. "Hey, Starshine, what's new? Done anything astounding yet?" He always called me Starshine, owing, I guess, to my rare astrological pedigree. "Not yet. How are you, Izzy?"

"Hanging on the ropes, kid—so your dad is abroad and doing well?"

"Yes, I'm glad he wrote to you," I said.

"He hasn't written me—I saw it in the stars." And I've always believed that he did.

## heaven points

Blind Danny lost his eyesight in South Korea in 1953, just two weeks short of the Korean War's end. He said a one-two punch of friendly fire and rotten luck caused the explosion that left him sightless on that fateful day. Back home, Danny had earned a living as a freelance photographer for girlie magazines. Now, unable to work in his former capacity and not possessing any other particular skills, he sort of gave up on living altogether. "All but the breathing and shitting parts" was how he put it.

I met him early in 1971 when he lived at the Hotel Knickerbocker just below Izzy the astrologer. On the walls hung evidence of his lost, dashing glory. In one photograph Danny sat behind the wheel of an MG convertible with a racing cap pulled down slick over one eye. Another picture showed him at Don the Beachcomber's, seated in a booth, a gorgeous woman on either side, tall exotic drinks lined up in front of them. Over the years since his accident, the Veterans Administration had made several attempts to send volunteers to help him with cooking and cleaning, but he always attacked them, and in the end they gave up, labeling him a hostile paranoid. Danny haunted the VA hospital, bombarding them with complaints of chronic, inexplicable pain until they finally wrote him a generous scrip for morphine just to get rid of him, which made Dad quite envious, though he quickly added, "Poor Danny—he's one of the unluckiest cats I know."

Dad and I visited Izzy every week or two, but the cat hair and cigar smoke became increasingly hard on my asthma, and Dad suggested I pay a visit to Blind Danny for an hour. "Offer to make him a sandwich or read him a book—you know, kindness earns you heaven points." He winked. Dad believed that enough good deeds would clinch you a spot in heaven. When I arrived at Danny's he had a stack of three paperbacks sitting on a cigarette-burned coffee table and asked that I choose one to read aloud to him. The first title, *The Four Horny Sisters*, I quickly set aside, only to find that *Hot Leather Seats* was my second choice. It had a lousy cover, and I pinned my hopes on the last book, *Case of the Throbbing Organ*. I thought it might be a *Hitchcock Presents* story, or something comic like *The Ghost and Mr. Chicken*, though once I scanned it, I saw it was cheap porn like the rest. I looked at Danny, who thought he was looking at me. He had the pathetic expression of a starved dog. Flipping through the yellowing pages, I decided it was a quick, easy read. What did I care? I'd just go home afterward and take a bath.

As I read aloud the empty words that meant nothing to me, I glanced over at smiling Danny, who was attempting to hide his whacking off with a frilly "I Love Florida" pillow that danced on his lap. My indifference soon changed into confused discomfort as I tried to decide if I was now racking up points in heaven or hell.

When Dad knocked on the door to collect me, I stuffed *The Throbbing Organ*, of which I'd read forty-two pages, under a cushion, not wishing to have my dad thrown in jail for murdering a blind man. "She sure reads well for a nine-year-old," Danny said. Dad looked at my proudly. "She likes to help people out." As the two of them stood talking at the door, I seized the opportunity to quickly move a stool in front of the entrance to the bathroom. Gram always said, "We all pay in this life. Everyone has to answer for their actions." I was looking for some assurance on that theory. Break your neck, Blind Danny, I thought. I'd still make it to heaven somehow.

# beauty of rain

Some cities have a particular season that best defines them, and for L.A., I always felt that it was summer. Most striking was how differently things sounded when filtered through the thick haze that would come in late June and stay through September. As a kid, I spent many summer afternoons with my head out the window, listening to Sly Stone being played on some distant cheap stereo along with the loud, lazy conversations of end-of-their-rope mothers and the sound of babies wailing in many languages, their cries rarely answered. Plastic wading pools meant for two or three sat in the middle of Hollywood courtyards, at least six wild kids piled into each, while neighbors looked on from behind broken screen doors and cats sat on top of rusted-out VWs on lawns of long-dead, overgrown grass.

My passion was for summer showers. Dad said my love of the rain came from being conceived and born on rainy days. To me the smell of rain-wet pavement was sweeter than that of any flower. I'd lie out on the fire escape, looking straight up at the sky's end, trying to see the rain's origin, watching it fall in seemingly slow motion, perfectly silent and true. Holy water. On the street below, shirtless boys skateboarded down slippery sidewalks with long, wet locks sticking to their backs, beautiful as statues.

Then there were the old people who hung out at the bus stops, never going anywhere, just sitting on the benches, watching. These ancient sentinels were a mystery to me.

Who were they? Had they been radicals or jewel thieves? Now they only sat at the Hollywood and Western or Hollywood and Vine bus stops, toothless and forlorn, with wet newspapers held over their withered heads, too old and tired to enjoy the rain. The summer showers never lasted long, but when they did come, I felt that life held possibilities, and I'd find myself almost believing in something.

## the poodle lover

It wasn't easy for a kid to make a buck in a hotel where few people ever had more than a nickel in their pockets, but at one point, I had a steady dog-walking job for an old widow named Mrs. Avery. She was a scary-looking woman, always dressed head to toe in black, including a black veil that hung over her hat and long black gloves, regardless of the weather. Her dog was an old standard poodle named Stein who had cataracts in both eyes and the foulest breath I've ever encountered. They'd move through the halls like ancient silent shadows, their combined ages easily topping two hundred, counting dog years. Every day at 5:00 PM I'd knock at room 212 to collect my fifty cents and Stein for our walk down the Boulevard, as far as Wilton Place and back. One particular Saturday, I arrived at 4:00 PM, hoping I could walk the dog early since Dad and I were going to the Star Theatre twilight matinee to see *Bananas*. I knocked on her door a couple of times, but received no reply, although I could hear that old song: "Somewhere just around the corner, there's a rainbow in the sky—so let's have another cup of coffee, and let's have another piece of pie" blasting on her phonograph.

I started to imagine that Mrs. Avery, and maybe Stein too, had "punched their tickets," as Dad used to say, and wondered if I should go seek help, or try to investigate myself. I opted for the latter, and found that the door was, unfortunately, unlocked. When I poked my head around the wall that separated the entranceway from the main room, I fell witness to a bizarre scene. Mrs. Avery was propped up on the bed, stark naked except for her hat and veil, singing to the music full tilt while her faithful canine shoved his head between her spindly white legs, nosing away at her nasty old cooze with great vigor. I stood glued in queasy fascination, trying to think of how I was going to get out of walking her perverted poodle ever again. I ducked out quietly and headed back to our room, where I composed the following letter: "Dear Mrs. Avery, Dogs make me sneeze now. Sorry I can't walk Styn. Amy Jo." She never tried to get in touch with me after that, only made the occasional appearance in my disturbed dreams. I felt a little badly— perhaps I had let her down, not helping out, but at least she wasn't totally alone. She had her pal Stein for company, which was more than a lot of people have.

# laundromat, 2001

There was a Laundromat on Western that I used to hang out in. It was open from 6:00 AM to midnight. The long hours and the fact that there was a sink made it a popular destination for the homeless, though the owner, Manny, never let anyone hang out too long. When he caught sight of one of them trying to wash out socks or stay warm in the early-morning L.A. chill by huddling near a dryer, he'd abruptly kick them out. "What the hell kinda place you think I'm runnin'?" he'd scream.

Manny looked like an unscrupulous fight promoter of old, with his Durante nose, stubby cigar, and moth-eaten suit and hat, long after the death of suits and hats. He'd open in the morning and polish everything to perfection. It was beautiful and immaculate, with all the most modern equipment, and triple-load washers that had blinding chrome front-loading doors. The ceiling even had the special stucco with silver sparkling bits in it. "That there is the deluxe stardust finish," he'd point out proudly to unhappy overworked housewives who didn't give a shit. Music was always piped in, what he called "Easy classicals. *Très* elite." When the place was empty of people, and I'd sit in its vast, gleaming whiteness listening to the music, I felt like I was in the movie *2001: A Space Odyssey*. Dad had taken me to see *2001* at the impressive Cinerama Dome when I was only six. I couldn't make sense of it but was riveted by the imagery, and I remember asking Dad after the movie how old I would be in 2001. "Hmmm—thirty-nine years old." I was devastated, certain I'd be dead before reaching such an advanced age. I wanted to live to see the fantastically sparse and silent future represented in that film.

The Laundromat, I feared, might be as close as I'd get. Manny bopped in and out of the place throughout the day and night, grumbling to himself about everything in a stream of obscenities. "Fucking bums—clean 'em up!" or "What's with these hairy fucking broads? Nothing a good hosing won't fix—ha!" He always made derogatory remarks about the feminist movement, which was making headlines in 1970. Perhaps because he sensed my appreciation for his fine establishment, I was the only non-coin-feeding loiterer who was allowed to stay.

One day as I watched an old woman struggling to fold her laundry, I offered to help, having grown bored with sitting around. To my delight, she rewarded me with a quarter tip when I'd finished. That's when I got the idea of charging to help people fold their laundry. Manny, pleased with my nine-year-old entrepreneurial spirit, took the matter to task, hanging a sign on the bulletin board that read: LAUNDRY FOLDING: 50 CENTS PER LOAD BETWEEN 3:30 AND 6:30 PM. We didn't have a phone at home, so Manny came up with the after-school hours. The bastard charged me half my profits to conduct business there. I had a lot of customers, but burned out after a few months. Summer was coming, and with the heat from the dryers, it felt like 120 degrees in there. This experience left me

with a permanent aversion to clothes folding. Now I stuff
everything straight from dryer to drawer. Won't even shake
them out. I made some money, anyway, and it kept me out
of trouble for a while.

## saints and sinners

We had some strange neighbors in Hollywood. A few were
old spinsters who felt compelled to offer me guidance,
whether I wanted it or not. One such lady was Mrs. Culver
("of the Culver City Culvers") who decided that the only
hope for me and my delinquency was to accept Jesus into
my heart. She asked my father if she could take me to her
Protestant church on Sunday, but he was wary: "Well, we're
Catholics—I wouldn't want to confuse her." However, she
persisted, and in the end prevailed. Bright and early one
Sunday, to church we went, accompanied by her greasy
nephew, Ernest, the kind of guy who was always jerking off
in the bushes when I walked to school.

My first impression, upon arrival, was that it was quite
an ugly church, and that all of the people in it were badly
dressed. Mrs. Culver hightailed it over to the preacher and
talked to him frantically, gesturing to me, who he glanced at
gravely a few times. Then began the endless hokey hymns
and droning sermons. Within minutes, I was light-years
away, but at some point I realized this alien on the pulpit
had homed in on me. "Friends, look upon this poor child

who is not in God's flock . . ." he began. Mrs. Culver and
Ernest then guided me by the elbows down the aisle toward the weird man of God, who was growing louder and
holding his arms out to me. The congregation stared, and
some wept audibly, at which point I decided I wouldn't be
sacrificed without a fight. I started screaming and tried to
make a break for it as the alien yelled, "Satan is taking hold
of the girl," and I thought, Pal, if Satan were to show up
now, I'd go flying happily into his red-hot arms to escape
this God-fearing freak show.

After much to-do that included a laying of clammy
hands upon my possessed and fevered brow, my torment
ended once I decided to give the preacher double shin
scrapes down both legs to remember me by.

When I arrived home, Dad took one look at me, in
hysterical overdrive, and said, "Oh, little Jo. I'm so sorry."
Mrs. Culver was standing back a little in the hallway looking sheepish. "Keep away from my daughter, you fucking
witch," said Dad, slamming the door as she said she would
pray for us both.

From that moment on I detested all organized religions,
though I still enjoyed reading about the lives of saints, like
Saint Agatha, who died on my birthday and was from Cat-
ania, just like my great-grandmother. A martyred virgin,
Saint Agatha was sodomized and had her nipples torn off
after refusing to let herself be deflowered by some high-
ranking Roman official. Such dedication to any belief truly
inspired me. I'd play a game called "Saints" in which I'd

test my pain threshold—poking myself with sharp objects, sticking my fingers in the fire, trying to make my palms bleed with sandpaper, et cetera. I concluded back then that it was wise to avoid overzealous Christians.

# jamming

I sometimes accompanied my dad to jam sessions that took place in the houses and bungalows—even one penthouse— of musicians and jazz fans all over Hollywood. It wasn't always as exciting as it may sound. Unless we were in the home of our friends Stan and Ellie, the atmosphere was usually not kid friendly. On many occasions I was greeted by some too-cool character groaning, "Shit, Joe, did you have to bring the kid?" to which Dad would simply say, "Fuck you," not being one to mince words. In the end they'd tolerate me because they knew they were fortunate to have Dad and his talent there to make them look good. These evenings sometimes deteriorated into enormous circle jerks. There were so many large egos awaiting their climax, the inevitable eight-bar solo, that the room could barely contain them.

I remember Dad telling me the story of working with Charlie Parker's group in 1946. A young Miles Davis was also featured in the group. They were rehearsing for a live radio airshot out of the Finale Club in L.A. Dad said: "I was accompanying Bird and having a hard time figuring out what he expected of me. I tried out a few different things, but when I'd look at him he just shook his head, 'no.' Frustrated, I turned the beat around [played the melody backward], hoping for approval. Still nothing. Finally I yelled, 'Fuck you, Bird!' and he said, 'You're fired, Joe!' then turned his back. Even so, I felt his eyes staring at me."

Dad would beat himself up endlessly over the incident, saying that he wasn't good enough to keep up. When I tried pointing out that other musicians had said Parker was difficult to play with, and he should cut himself some slack, I got the brush-off. He preferred, in true Catholic form, always to lay blame with himself, especially when it came to the alto sax god Parker. Once I made the mistake of saying I enjoyed listening to Lester Young over Charlie Parker, which solicited the response: "What the hell do you know?" It was true, I only knew what I liked, but in the often too-serious jazz scene, it seems what one likes isn't valid unless backed up by a twenty-page dissertation. That attitude probably accounts for a certain percentage of jazz enthusiasts who are pedantic bores.

There was an odd mix at these scenes. You had your goateed, spectacled set in their twenties, who sat off in a corner reading the writings of Lenin, and the weekend hipsters, who'd waltz in from the Palisades for a naughty night of Hollywood debauchery. It seemed to me that the women around were viewed merely as pretty baubles, good for collecting bottles and emptying ashtrays, which was a grave injustice. Some remarkable women gravitated to that scene. There was Ellie, a talented painter who possessed a kindness so genuine it often filled me with sadness. Then there was fast-talking Jean. Jean Roth, who started as Irma Rothman, had been a gorgeous Dior model when Dad met her in the middle '40s on Fifty-Second Street. Fifty-Second Street, between Fifth and Seventh Avenues, was the nucleus of the jazz universe then. "You could step out of one club and duck into another that was right next door. It was like gorging yourself on a fabulous two-block-long smorgasbord." That was the preface for one of my dad's many bedtime stories about Fifty-Second Street, where he attained musical enlightenment on several occasions.

When Dad played at these jam sessions, I would plant myself near the piano and marvel, along with everyone else, at his flying fingers and stomping feet. He was very physical, like Monk, in his approach. Dad liked to sit high above the keyboard; even at six feet, he would often put a phone book on the bench in order to "get on top of things." Sometimes when he really got going, he'd grunt and groan (which posed a problem for one French recording engineer when they got into the studio). He sweated profusely and, I thought, gave the piano dirty looks when he played.

I'd always wish that he was playing solo, and I was right on the bench next to him, listening to "Wait Till You See Her" or some other favorite song. I'll never profess to understand the exact space that music occupied in his life. He tended to cover his devotion to music. I only know he preferred playing solo, and that he worshipped the music of

Ellington, Arlen, Strayhorn, and others excessively, to the detriment perhaps of his own songwriting potential.

## eddie no-collar

Father Eddie Calardi, or "Eddie No-Collar," as Dad called him, was an excommunicated priest. Eddie, Dad, and many of their friends congregated at a bar that once lived on the corner of Hollywood Boulevard and Gramercy Place. Father Eddie could tell you which saint's day it was on any given day of the year, though I'm not sure if his answers were always legit. Sometimes I'd catch him off guard, sneaking up from behind: "Hey, Father, whose saint's day is it?" The poor man, deep in religious meditation, would jump, spilling his Jim Beam everywhere, but after a moment's thought, he always came up with an answer: "February 8—Saint Jerome was born today in 1481, Venice, Italy. Italians, naturally are the best saints. He was named the patron saint of orphans in 1928, canonized 1767, died while caring for the sick on his fifty-sixth birthday. Let's drink to Saint Jerome! Georgie, my son, encore." He held up his empty glass to the bartender, who told him his tab was getting out of hand. "Ah, well. Just one more, George?" he asked ruefully. George invariably came over with a fresh Jim Beam, and a Shirley Temple for me.

Father Eddie looked like Dean Martin, who I was in love with at the time, though he was an older, more wizened version. He even held his lowball glass and cigarette in the same hand, like Martin, always up in a toast, ready to absolve the sins of his fellow alcoholics, who stumbled into his red leather confessional booth both day and night.

I asked him once why he didn't belong to a parish anymore. Placing a heavy hand on my head, he told the following tale. "Do you know the demon called Asmodeus?" I shook my head as best I could, with it compressed under the deadweight of his hand. "Asmodeus is the fiery demon of lust. One night he visited me in the guise of a piteous, painted woman." His hand trembled as he paused to drink. "She fixed me with eyes that turned crimson, and I was paralyzed. My soul, at least, impotent. Well, I've said too much now." It was a strange story that meant nothing to me at the time.

It wasn't long before Father Eddie stopped coming to the bar. One day Dad asked George if he had news. George looked at me, and Dad handed over a dime for the jukebox to get me out of earshot, unaware of my supersonic hearing. "Dementia. Eddie's been under a doctor's care for years. He stopped taking his medication, and that combined with the booze . . ." George gave a thumbs-down sign. Dad shook his head gravely. Apparently Eddie went to the Olympic to watch the fights. Midway though a lightweight bout, he got the notion that this one boxer was possessed. "He jumped in the ring and stabbed this poor kid in the eye with a rosary—almost put his eye out. Anyway, he's over in the psychiatric ward—county," George said.

"Christ, what a lousy deal," Dad said, sipping on a ginger ale. I guess all that piety and compassion made for conflicted bedfellows. The church lost a devoted priest when they ousted Father Eddie. A religious scholar and a great, mad lush.

## baseball

The Helms Bakery man came once a week, his truck filled with fresh donuts you could smell from a half a block away. Whenever he spotted me coming, he'd pull out the tray of giant glazed twists. They were the stuff of dreams. One morning, while sitting on the curb enjoying a warm twist, I felt a sharp burning sensation in my legs, and looking down, discovered that I was sitting on an army of angry fire ants. I launched into a frenzy that only ended after a cold bath followed by a dousing of calamine lotion.

Dad, feeling badly about my half-eaten legs, surprised me with a present. It was the orange softball bat, ball, and mitt that I'd been eyeing in the window of the Hollywood Toy Store. We started going to a nearby church parking lot a few afternoons a week to play ball. As a kid, Dad had been a pretty good ball player, and would have pursued it—that or boxing. He was fast, agile, with a great reach, but Grandpop insisted that all his spare time be devoted to accordion lessons, which he hated.

Sometimes, when we played ball, the two of us seemed to find a rhythm. The bat kept connecting, and seemingly

impossible catches were made, one after another, all beneath the perfect light and warmth of the late-afternoon
sun. It was an unspeakably corny bliss. During these times,
I felt that my life was simple and ordinary, in the best possible way. It was overcast on the day that I pitched one
straight on target, and Dad swung at it hard, sending the
ball sailing, and ultimately crashing through a stained-glass
church window. I looked around, nervous, awaiting a lesson
in correct behavior for just such a circumstance, when Dad
grabbed my arm: "Run for it—run!" We took off, looking
behind us, expecting a mad mob of priests to be hot on our
trail, but it was all clear. I hoped to find another lot to play
in, scouted around, and made some suggestions, but Dad's
interest had waned, and my few weeks of masquerading as
a regular kid came to an abrupt end. It was difficult for Dad
to maintain any positive habits; only bad habits received his
vigilant attention, because they demanded it. The bat and
glove are long gone, but I'll always have the scar on my el-
bow where I snagged it on a chain-link fence while making
a fine flying catch. It's the proudest scar on my entire body.

## the miraculous

Miracles, I was certain, could occur only within the first
two hours after sunup, and I woke every day at 5:00 AM,
bursting with a sense of miraculous possibilities. As the
day wore on and faded to evening, so faded my hopes that

something spectacular would transpire. However, with the next day's dawning, all bets were back on, and after lying in bed awhile, listening to familiar sounds of the city stretching its careworn limbs, I'd dress and head down to Hollywood Boulevard on my holy quest. At the age of nine, I was religious on this matter, for Izzy the astrologer had foreseen that great luck would come to me in my ninth year and smile, he promised, "long and hard."

It was like a ghost town that early when I walked through the piss-drenched underpass at Hollywood and Wilton, a risky proposition in itself, then continued west past the Salvation Army, which always had a soul or two huddled by its door, a few steps closer to God. Next came the closed-down Florentine Gardens Supper Club, where Dad had played the accordion as a teenager fresh from New Jersey, and where Grandpop had been a waiter. I'd cross over, make my way past the Blue Chip Stamp store and Chicken Delight, feeling more alive as I approached Hollywood and Vine. On the southeast corner was a small newspaper stand run by a guy who'd been there for over twenty years. At one time, he'd sold papers to some of the big stars, and would always offer a story, since he knew of my fondness for old movies. "Spencer Tracy was a real good guy, always said: 'Here's a tip for ya, Mack.' And Joan Crawford"—he whistled through his teeth and rolled his eyes—"very grand, with a handshake like Joe Louis."

The newspaper man, who I guess I'll call Mack, not knowing his name, eventually moved up the Boulevard to an office-building lobby, where he grudgingly sold candy and aspirin along with the occasional paper. "People don't read anymore," he complained. Last time I saw him, I was about fifteen, and sporting a head of violet-colored hair. Mack looked at me wearily: "Ah. What happened, honey? You lose a bet?" I felt suddenly self-conscious and weak-minded. "Yeah, you guessed it," I answered, thinking I'd lost a bet with myself that I could exist forever as an island.

I don't know what became of Mack, but I always felt they should have given him a star on the Walk of Fame. He was certainly more significant than most of the people who've received one over the last twenty years.

I would continue up the street pondering the eerie loneliness of the Lerner's store window mannequins, and imagined what the Boulevard must have been like in years past, when men like Cary Grant and women in Lily Dasche hats had strolled down the once-glittering pavement. The old Janes House fascinated me. It was a foreboding Gothic-style place that had two tall turrets framed by giant palm trees. It was the only house between Vine and Highland, and had been a private school for the likes of Charlie Chaplin's and Mary Pickford's kids, among others, run by two spinster sisters whose last name was Jane. I'd heard rumors that *What Ever Happened to Baby Jane?* had been somehow inspired by the old house and its mysterious sisters, which greatly added to its creepy mystique.

One morning I knocked on the front door, then ran behind a palm tree to see, I suppose, what would happen.

From one of the upper windows, a pale hand pulled back lace curtains, and a frail face peered out and looked around in desperation, as if searching for the company of a long-dead companion. My eyes filled with tears, and I was gripped with a terrible sense of guilt over my mischievous prank. It crossed my mind that I too could end up in solitude among nothing but cobwebs and trinkets, like Miss Havisham in *Great Expectations*. My journey continued as far as Grauman's Chinese Theatre, where I drifted from footprint to handprint, alone with Hollywood history, except for the occasional jet-lagged tourist who wandered at odd hours, camera in hand, trying to figure out why Hollywood didn't look anything like the travel brochures or celluloid images they were accustomed to seeing.

Even in the early seventies, I thought that if you looked hard enough, you could still see something of what it might have been. Not anymore, though. Now it's deader than a cadaver that's had its head caved in with a club, just for good measure. Every cheap gold-sprayed statue that's erected is another blow to the corpse's head. My ninth year came and went, and though it seemed to me at the time that luck hadn't even stopped long enough to blink in my general direction, I grew to understand that sometimes luck is simply the privilege of seeing another sunup and having the chance to wait, ever expectant, for something miraculous to happen.

# a walk in the park

My father and I spent a lot of time walking to Fern Dell, a park in the middle of Hollywood, right off Western and Los Feliz. Fern Dell was a haven for social outcasts, hippies, homeless folk. Sometimes we'd be accompanied by a couple of Dad's friends—Bob Whitlock, Art Pepper, or Lester Hobbs (a trumpet player who had two fingers missing on his right hand, the result of shooting up in his hand, having exhausted all other veins). It was interesting to see the way these original hepcats adapted to the style of the times. They all had sideburns, longer hair, paisley shirts with big lapels, flares—but they still shined their shoes. All in their late forties, at the time, they were still the coolest.

One Sunday, we headed to Fern Dell with Art and Lester and two friends of mine, Gerald and Lorna, the black albino siblings. They looked pretty strange, with their big white afros and pink eyes like white rabbits. The other kids at my new school were terrified of them, due in great part to the fact that the movie *The Omega Man* had just come out, and everyone thought they were atomic zombies. They cleared the hallways. *The Omega Man* was playing at the Star Theatre with *Billy Jack*—a kid's dream double bill in 1971. I, being the official friend of the friendless, hooked up with Gerald and Lorna when the three of us got socked away together in corrective—or "retarded," as the other kids called it—PE. I was there because of my asthma, and they were in with light- and heat-sensitivity problems.

There we were at Fern Dell that Sunday, three jazz junkies, two black albinos, and me, along with loads of flower children, people playing recorders, dogs, and naked babies. Dad had just bought me a portable six-inch Sony TV that came with a battery pack larger than the television itself. We decided to take it to the park for a test run. *The Brain That Wouldn't Die* was on *Chiller*, which was my favorite show. This TV must have been one of the first portables, judging from the excitement it generated. We ended up with a dozen people crowded around this six-inch screen, smoking pot and watching *Chiller*. Dad, Lester, and Art were having wasted laughing fits, making dumb jokes about getting head from the severed head of the woman in the movie.

This was the same day that Dad met a free spirit named Melodie. Melodie attracted the attention of Dad and every other male, as she danced with a tree, wearing only a few colorful chiffon scarves that she'd tied into a makeshift dress. She lived in a commune over on Van Ness. Very pretty and very strange, Melodie ate cat food and had a son my age who'd shit in the old tires in their backyard. One week after this *Chiller*-in-the-park lovefest, Dad hocked my beloved TV set. I remember feeling angry with him for the first time. It was then that I realized that no love, however deep, remains unspoiled forever.

# christmas at the st. francis

Christmas was a time to hone my shoplifting skills, and the Broadway Hollywood department store was a fairly easy mark. The place crawled with undercover store security, but they weren't hard to spot, with their stiff mannerisms and shifty eyes. They are society's reigning bottom-feeders.

My technique was not particularly original. I would simply palm the desired item, and with a push of my fingertips, send it up my sleeve. The trick was to keep the left hand busy picking up merchandise in an assured and visible manner while the right hand quietly "palmed and pushed" the true object of interest. The obvious drawback to this method was the size limitation it imposed, though it's surprising what one can fit in a large sleeve. I'd take lighters, cuff links, ties, handkerchiefs, and cologne for my dad, and even managed smaller mass-market paperbacks and some Chinese slippers for Gram, who wore them all year round. Dad naïvely believed that my dog-walking and odd-job money was enough to explain the rather pricey gifts he'd find in his Christmas stocking.

Although we'd usually spend the holidays with Gram, I remember one Christmas spent at our St. Francis digs with a few other lonely misfits. We had a tree made of tinsel that looked like an accident, with blue frosted lights and a large clef note made of foil perched on top. Dad bought me *Charlie Parker with Strings* and *The Complete Works of Shakespeare*, which was a little rough to digest at nine, but

I did enjoy *A Midsummer Night's Dream*, having loved the movie with James Cagney and Joe E. Brown. Each of our five guests brought a stack of records, and for once, there was plenty of food. Two double hot plates and a toaster oven managed to create a sizable feast. Lester came dressed as a smacked-out, chain-smoking, three-fingered Santa, which was a dead giveaway to his identity.

Dad danced around in his inimitable, fabulous fashion. I've only met one other guy who could dance half as cool, and he too was an Italian musician from Jersey. It was a style born of complete abandon and utter rhythmic confidence. I could dance with Dad for hours. There were four other musicians present that evening, and the conversation soon turned itself over to passionate debates on all matters musical. I'd always try to absorb what was discussed in these situations, realizing that I was privy to some musical genius.

As the night wore on, a quiet tension hung in the air, and I sensed that it was time for me to retire for the evening so the grown-ups could get high. As I closed my eyes and faked sleep, I heard Dad admonishing Lester, "Hey, man—you can't use that tie. A.J. just bought me that for Christmas!"

## jolly beans

One of Dad's best friends was Dalton, a fascinating guy who made porno movies for a living. From what I gathered, he was quite a talented filmmaker. They had met years earlier at an after-hours club on the Strip where fellow hipsters like Lenny Bruce, Terry Southern, Joe Maini, and others would get together after 2:00 AM to talk, goof off, mostly listen to music.

In the spring of '71, Dad was in trouble with the law again. To hear him tell it, he had tried to cop, Mickey Mouse showed, and he got twisted and violated. In English, he was buying dope, the cops showed, and he was sentenced for the buy and for violating his parole. Most of the grown-ups around me spoke in a sort of code.

Instead of standing sentence, we laid low at Dalton's, and I soon learned the language of blue movies. Any innocence I had left would soon be gone. Dalton's house was in North Hollywood, and he had a son a couple of years older than me named Monty. There was a large detached back house where some films were shot. During our stay Dalton was working on a series of "sexual enlightenment" films: "Real bon-a-roo sex education," he'd say. Monty and I were always spying through the windows at the weird and wondrous sights. I saw an Indian guru performing auto-fellatio and auto-anal sex. There were demonstrations concerning the attainment of various orgasms. Fusion, tantric, altered states—after the initial shock wore off, all the writhing, moaning nakedness seemed commonplace.

The house was filled with books and "sexual research" papers. Being an avid reader, I was kept busy reading everything I could get my hands on. Monty and I made up a dirty word game, the object being who could come up with the most genital slang words: *snapper, cooze, lizard, short arm, quim, rod, snatch, box*. I can't remember them all now, but I usually triumphed.

During this time Dad was quite happy. He had a piano to play, plenty of hash and other intoxicants, and women galore. Dalton was always hooking him up. He'd say, "Ladies, you are in the presence of greatness. This is the legendary Joe Albany." Women really went for my dad. I think it had to do with this very sweet, almost old-fashioned quality he possessed. I remember walking in on him and Dalton with two skin-flick starlets while he was reciting that poem "I think that I shall never see a poem as lovely as a tree." The girls were all giggles and coos, and Dalton, stoned as usual, was saying, "That's beautiful, man."

There was a big buzz going around about some little blue pills that everyone referred to as "jolly beans." They seemed to make whoever took them terribly happy, and since I liked the name, I snaked one out of its hiding place and tried it. That was the day I fell in love with speed. Like Icarus flying on high, drunk with a sense of invincibility, and like the best-ever carnival ride, speed was a blast, until you fell to earth, the ride ended, and you were left feeling sick and broken.

When the time came to leave Dalton's, it was—as usual—sudden, and the reasons why unclear. I'd become accustomed to our transitory life and no longer wasted time asking questions. It seemed to be our destiny to stay on the move, like unhappy sharks.

# alain

Alain looked like the illustration of D'Artagnan in my copy of *The Three Musketeers*. When he smiled, it was the brilliant Technicolor smile of Errol Flynn in *Robin Hood*. He was beyond dashing. He was the first-ever object of my desire, and he was only forty-eight inches tall. Although his head was not misshapen—on the contrary, it was unearthly beautiful—and his torso was proportioned, he had the short arms and small bowed legs that are common in most dwarfs.

I met him at Dalton's, where he was starring in one of Dalton's art-porno flicks. His life was one of unspeakable sadness and adventure that made my own problems seem so relatively small, you'd need a microscope to spot them. His father was a religious zealot who believed that his son's deformity was an indication of God's displeasure with Alain's mother, who he beat regularly. He also attempted to stretch his son on a self-styled rack, which Alain endured until the age of eleven, at which time he ran away and hooked up with a Danish carnival that featured a troupe of performing dwarfs.

He spent the next seven years traveling the world. On the road, he was introduced to morphine to help with the almost constant pain that his body was in, and became what he called a "medicinal user." He could recite Romantic poetry in four languages, had a splendid singing voice, was an impressive magician, and was tragically unhappy.

He lived on Bronson, just off Franklin Avenue, which was ten to twelve blocks away from the St. Francis, where we were once again living. I would ride my bike over to his apartment with my father's approval, since he believed that all females, clowns, people in animal costumes, and anyone shorter than myself were harmless companions for me.

Perhaps I was a sick and devious nine-year-old to be so enamored of a twenty-two-year-old morphine-addicted porno-movie dwarf. It's a possibility that I have always been comfortable with. In Alain's room was the waist-down half of a male mannequin, dressed in slacks with big shoes. He'd climb up onto the top of the mannequin's waist and put on a large jacket that he'd button around the dummy's front. "Look! I am a normal man now." I was unimpressed, and re-member thinking, I would adore you no more at eighty-two inches than I do at forty-eight inches. However, Alain was mesmerized by this image. His mannequin was strategically placed in front of a full-length mirror, where I imagine he spent hours staring at his impossible fantasy. My own guard-ed fantasy was made public after a creature named Nadine, who Dad was knocking around with, found my journal and read it aloud in front of Dad and his friends, Lou and Art. "Alain my love, I long for the day our lips meet, and we run away on a silvery horse and . . ." Dad silently snatched the book away from her as I slunk, horrified, into the bathroom, where I pressed my ear against the door, fearing the possibil-ity of my father's anger. For a while, there was silence, then Lou spoke: "Ha! That's cute. Kids are something else."

"Well, I'd keep them apart. Isn't there a word for people who like midgets?"

"He's a dwarf, and fuck you, Nadine. She's an empathetic kid—always for the underdog, picks out the runt of the litter."

"Oh, sure, no worries, man—she's a sweet kid."

Awkward silence.

"Maybe she needs professional help."

"Shut up, or maybe you'll need medical help, Nadine."

"He is a nice midget, though."

"A dwarf."

"Right. What's the difference, anyway?"

"Well, I think she's looking for, you know, attention."

"I give her attention."

"Oh, sure, I didn't mean—"

More silence.

"What's with the silver horse?"

"There's no such animal, is there?"

"Nadine, you're a fucking moron."

After more silence, Art spoke up. "All right—so who's holding tonight? Empty your pockets, gentlemen."

That was my cue to call it a night. In a few minutes, they'd be in the stratosphere. I grabbed Dad's robe off the back of the door, rolled up a towel for a pillow, and went to sleep in the tub. Sometime during the night, Dad picked me up and put me on the sofa bed. Next morning I kept a low profile, nose buried in my copy of *The Three Musketeers* with a now-altered drawing of a very short D'Artagnan. In the afternoon, I decided I would go to see Alain for the last time. Dad was brooding like a hurt child, as he always did when I upset him, and I could not bear it. I told him I was riding my bike over to the market. He regarded me with suspicion. "One hour, no more."

When I arrived at Alain's he looked amused, and I figured he had heard about the journal, since everyone shared the same drug connection. After one last look at the dark blue eyes and chestnut hair that curled around his glorious face, I told him I could see him no more. Before he had a chance to answer, and with a weird confidence I must have stolen from Cupid, I bent forward deeply from the waist, having been a polite distance back from the door as to not appear needlessly tall, and offered my lips as I had seen done a hundred times in old movies, prepared for my first kiss. He was sweetly accommodating, and something like electric liquid traveled down my body, startling me. I fled down the hall and onto my silvery bike-horse, leaving a trail of luminous blossoms that stretched all the way back to the St. Francis.

## the stuttering boy

Bunky had a terrible stutter. The stutter became apparent around the age of six, when Tex, his stepfather, first entered his life. Dad called Tex a "soulless yahoo," among other things, adding disdainfully: "He's a pillhead too—strung out on Percodan of all things." Dad didn't have much use for southerners, having had a number of negative experiences with them each time he toured down South. The first time was when he played with, I believe, Benny Carter's band, and the KKK tried to turn over the tour bus. On another occasion, he was in the company of Max Roach when they were refused service at a lunch counter. Dad threw a fit that almost landed him in jail.

Tex definitely gave Texans a bad name. For years, he had been throwing his stepson against the wall like some oversized handball. He also terrorized Bunky's mother and anybody who had the misfortune of crossing his path. Bunky and his mom walked the halls of the St. Francis with nervous, dark-circled eyes, their shoulders hunched high, as if they expected an anvil to drop on their heads at any moment. The first time I ever spoke to Bunky was up on the roof, where we would seek refuge from the drama of life down below. From atop the St. Francis, you could see much of sprawling Tinseltown, from a distance sufficient to make it all appear shining and beautiful.

Viewed at street level, its beauty became lousy with an overabundance of flaws. Only thirteen years old, Bunky had the defeated aura of a sad old man. Each time I saw him, he had a new evident injury. We'd share a stolen cigarette, and usually didn't have much to say. To engage him in conversation seemed a little cruel; it took him a long time to work out a sentence.

One afternoon, when he appeared with a split lip and purple eye, I asked him why he stuck around. "You're old enough to take off," I said, rather foolishly. Even his sigh was a stutter. "I should have run away the day I was born. Now it's too late." I knew what he meant. Bunky often gazed intently in a southeasterly direction. Once I asked what he was looking for. "Arkansas. It's out over that way, somewhere." Bunky's family had come to L.A. from Arkansas five years earlier, in pursuit of the elusive golden dream that might or might not exist here, at the end of the world. Since then, Bunky's mom had been waitressing at Schwab's on Sunset, and Tex had become a full-time loser. After a while, Bunky had given up on school; the kids hassled him so relentlessly about his stutter.

There finally came a day when Bunky's mom, tired of being a human heavy bag, packed up, took her son, and went down to the Vine Street Greyhound station, where they caught a bus for home. When Tex was lucid enough to realize he'd been left high and dry, he went on a rampage, screaming down the halls, banging on everyone's door. He banged on our door, yelling: "Hey, kid, where did they go? I bet Bunky told you."

Dad was furious at this intrusion: "Beat it, you shit-kicking, cow-fucking mook." Dad had a great way with words. Eventually, the cops showed up and carted Tex off. The next morning, I headed up to the roof at five thirty, my favorite time of day. I looked southeast, out beyond Fern Dell, as Bunky had done, and for some reason I cried, though my thoughts were about how pleased I felt for him. He had made it out, and though I didn't know a damn thing about Arkansas, I was certain he'd be better off there. "Run, Bunky, run!" I yelled from the rooftop. Then I smiled. My time to escape would also come.

## out of towners

The L.A. *Free Press* was a local paper that sold for a quarter and could be found all over town in the late sixties, early seventies. The paper's demise occurred around the same time the concepts of peace and freedom became passé. These and a handful of other human virtues lost out to self-obsession and a manic desire to obtain as many possessions as possible. In the back of the *Free Press*, there was a personals column that always included letters from desperate parents searching for their runaway children: "Judy— Please come home, I won't make you go to school. I miss you. Love, Mom." Or, "Billy—I don't care what you've done, just please call your mother, she's worried sick." Et cetera, et cetera.

The fate of most of these lost teens and preteens wasn't very pretty. They hustled, stole, got hung up on drugs. Sometimes they were murdered, their bodies disposed of off Angeles Crest and other desolate stretches of highway. There was a girl, Janyce, who met her end starring in a snuff film. She went into it like a kamikaze pilot, knowing full well what would happen. Her only stipulation was that a copy of the film be sent to her mother and stepfather, who'd destroyed her with years of sexual and physical abuse. Her sometime-boyfriend, Johnny, who I knew as a regular Boulevard fixture from my own wanderings, told me of Janyce's end with a surprising air of detachment. Apparently he and a few other local kids had bets on whether she'd actually go through with it or not. "Goddamn," Johnny exclaimed after telling his story. Finally, some remorse, I thought. Just as I was going to offer a word of sympathy, Johnny said: "I lost twenty dollars betting she wouldn't do it. That bitch." I walked away word-lessly, reminding myself never to talk with him again.

The kids who descended on L.A. came from every cor-ner of the U.S. They'd hitchhike or bus in from Detroit, Tennessee, North Dakota, everywhere and nowhere, with wild delusions about Hollywood and the fame and riches that awaited all God's children who entered the city limits. I knew a guy named Willie, thin, with acne and big eyes, a Kentucky boy, who said he'd spent a whole week down at the beach and never once saw the Banana Splits riding in their dune buggy. "That's why I came here," he said ear-nestly. "Everyone on the TV looked like they were having so much fun. I sure wasn't." Willie was one of the legions of the disillusioned who roamed the Boulevard, hanging outside the Two Guys pizza place or Orange Julius, any-where, looking for handouts and affection. Some acted tough while others were visibly frightened.

As sad as it was, I felt just as sorry for my city. L.A. be-came an overburdened mother who couldn't care for all her wayward children. The world looked to her with a thousand glittering, impossible expectations that couldn't be lived up to. The crime rate between '69 and '72 quadrupled as all the disappointed transplants began to explode. I wanted to say: "Wise up. No one owes you anything, and even if they do, odds are they'll never pay up. Go back to Palookaville if you can't hack it." Anyway, they stayed, and many more came. They trashed my hometown, and it suffocated under the weight of their anger and ignorance. Hollywood was beaten beyond recognition. It would never recover, but I would never leave.

## king for a day

Dad rarely looked too hard or too long at the madness of his own addiction, but he often lamented the toll drugs took on the lives of his friends. Around 1985, he was playing somewhere—maybe at Sweet Basil in New York City—when an extremely down-and-out Chet Baker came in. Dad and Chet had known and, surprisingly, even liked each other for almost forty years, though they hadn't met up since the early seventies, when both were playing a jazz festival in Europe. Chet approached Dad and asked if he could spot him a little cash, as he was at a real low end, and God knows it wasn't easy "to find one kind face in all of cold fucking New York," as Dad used to say. At that point, however, Dad had hit rock bottom himself, sometimes barely making it through the few gigs that still came his way. "Chet, you know I'd spot you if I had the bread, but I spent my advance and don't even have cab fare home. You're welcome to crash at my pad tonight." Chet took Dad's hands and squeezed them. "Thanks, Joe. You're a sweet guy." Dad was looking at a reflection of his own devastation, and told me that at that moment, he felt like crying. In the land of poor, blind Chet, my one-eyed Dad was king on that particular night.

A week later could have seen the situation reversed. At least Chet had experienced fame, a real celebrity that was usually reserved for pop stars. A great part of it was the James Dean good looks of his youth, and a willingness, to some extent, to play the game. Why, just once, couldn't Dad have swallowed his pride and allowed himself to be gawked at by the curious who would gladly pay to see what the wreckage of a once-great jazzman looked like? Chet and Dad could have traveled together as a sideshow act: "Step up and see the once-handsome and –talented great white hopes of the jazz world." There were a hundred other guys who could have gone on that tour too—the pianist Dodo Marmarosa, for one. Dad's oversensitivity and paranoia crippled him. He couldn't hear praise without feeling certain it was tinged with an underlying mockery. A young Frenchman came up to Dad on a Paris street once and asked for his autograph. "Why?" Dad said suspiciously. "Because you're the legendary Joe Albany, right?"

"Well, really? You think?" Dad mumbled, and shifted awkwardly like a kid, finally taking the guy's pen and scrawling an extensive declaration of his appreciation for the kind attention. Someone would have had to knock Dad over the head with a fat collection of all the great reviews he'd garnered and well-respected recordings he'd made before he'd accept the significance of his place in jazz history. He'd traveled far from his beginnings as an accordion-playing kid from New Jersey. Lester Young said he was "the best white pianist I ever laid eyes on," and when Charlie Parker couldn't get Bud Powell, Dad was his next-favorite choice. He also had the rare honor of being one of the few pianists not to be booted off the bench by Monk after Monk heard him play his composition "Ruby, My Dear." In the end, none of it seemed to mean much to him. His accomplishments never brought him much happiness.

Three years after their last meeting in that New York club, Joe Albany and Chet Baker would die within a few months of each other. Confidence or lack of, West Coast or hard bop, straight hair or curly, none of it had ever mattered. For both of them, musical obsession was their driving joy and staying high their tragic undoing in the end.

part three

# separating

By the end of '71, Dad was boxed into a bad corner filled with cops, pushers, and psychos. All over town, people were after him with various axes to grind. Around Christmas 1971, Dad was contacted by an English music promoter who said he could keep him working in Europe, book him into all the jazz festivals. Since work seemed to have dried up in L.A., Dad took him up on his offer and split for England. Over the next eight years, I would join him for brief periods. We lived in Denmark for a while and got to see a lot of Dexter Gordon, who I adored, but never again would it be just us two, each surviving for the sake of the other.

After Dad left, I lived with my grandmother. The general consensus was that, at nine, it would be good for me to settle into a normal life, but a normal life held little appeal. On the day I went to the airport to see him off, he was upbeat, and he said he'd send for me as soon as possible. We said goodbye, and I was watching him walk toward the plane when he spun around and yelled, "Ace-one-boon-white-coon, you're the nuttiest!" and then he was gone, and I felt my spirit drop out the bottom of my shoes, rarely to be seen again. This was the first time Dad ever left me behind by choice, and it put me in a mild state of shock. When the shock wore off, loneliness set in, and left me hard around the edges.

The only joyful thing I did around this time was to start collecting records. I bought the Velvet Underground and the *Clockwork Orange* soundtrack, and I stole *Led Zeppelin III* and the Stones' *Their Satanic Majesties Request*, figuring the latter two bands didn't need the money as much—ever a thief with a conscience. Dad left me his jazz LPs, but now I forged out on my own, musically.

While he was in Europe, his career took off. After so many years when he went unrecorded, he released a lot of LPs. It made me feel like I had somehow kept him down when he was with me. Not quite a jinx, but certainly no good luck charm. On the other hand, I felt I had been deserted. I had often sacrificed my own childhood to play parent to him, but perhaps he had sacrificed his art to play parent to me. I became a mass of pissed-off rebellion: boys, petty crime, drugs—all the usual suspects.

## losing it

In 1972, a correspondence began between my grandmother and my mother's sister, who lived in San Francisco. It was arranged that I would travel up north for visits four times a year to acquaint myself with the "other" side of the family, and perhaps fill some of the hole left by my father's departure.

I began menstruating at ten, had an extravagant bust size by eleven, and at the age of twelve, during one of my Frisco visits, was seduced by my mother's kid brother, Uncle John, who was twenty-one years old. There were those who knew and did nothing. Tragic, all the dirty little secrets we allow to live comfortably on our backs. These sexual episodes continued for many years until, with the help of lots of amphetamines, I found sufficient confidence to tell him I wanted it to end. After I said my piece, he looked at me with anger, and perhaps some fear, then jumped on his motorcycle and drove wildly away without a word. That evening, a call came to my aunt's house. John had lost control of his bike and crashed into a concrete retaining wall, dying on impact, his neck broken. I wasn't sure how I should feel. For a moment, I felt I was to blame, but that passed quickly. There were others who felt that was the case and let me know it by their expressions of extreme distaste or by the way they'd refuse to look at me at all, but I was never one to back the popular opinion.

## brothers

Somewhere in my twelfth year, I began to lose faith. Dad was far away, and it seemed I'd lost myself when I lost my virginity. Life was looking like a sucker bet that would never pay off. Entering junior high was the last shabby straw.

Le Conte Junior High doubled as a pharmacy back then. Baggies of whites and black beauties were easily obtained at a good price. My school was also a hangout for half the gangs in L.A.—Rebels, Clantone, Crips, Bloods. There was a fight every day, and the cops were ineffectual. Around this time, I became friendly with two brothers— Tommy, fifteen, and Johnny, sixteen. They lived in a di-lapidated house on Garfield between Franklin Avenue and Hollywood Boulevard. Both were on probation, with arrest records as long as their waist-length hair. I spent the spring of '74 hanging around watching them work on an old Mus-tang they planned to drive across the country. Cruel spring: it lies lightly on the surface of your skin and fills you with unattainable desires. I lusted after both boys with equal de-votion, to no avail. I felt certain that if I could persuade either brother to sleep with me, I'd have a shot at cleansing the creeping stench of incest that made me feel like a mon-ster. However, these boys were noble as knights. Besides, I was so pimply and insecure at the time, my chances were decidedly slim.

In late July, they moved away, in search of a father long lost who was doing time in some Detroit pen. They took their Black Sabbath records, angel dust, and astonishing beauty with them. I was shattered. I started cutting class more often, ducking into shops when the truant police drove by. A root beer float at the Woolworth lunch counter was my usual start-ing point. I'd make my way over to the Orient shop, attempt-ing to lift something while the inscrutable proprietor watched me like a hawk. Vogue Records and Books was the next stop, and my journey always ended at the Pickwick Bookshop.

It was a two-story heaven where one could get lost all day. I'd learn more in a few hours there than in two semesters at school. Though I still attended a couple of classes that were of interest to me—art and American literature—I stopped wasting my time with the likes of math and California history, which was surely the most boring course known to man. With my daily routine firmly established, I found a way to drift awkwardly through the minefields of adolescence.

## the proposition

The route I took to junior high was a short but perilous one. All the local perverts were clued in to the paths traveled by young schoolgirls. There was a desolate stretch that ran along the freeway on Wilton Place by radio station KTLA that was a prime location in which to be accosted.

One May morning, as I plodded along trying to decide whether I'd last another month and make it past the seventh grade, I became aware of someone walking beside me. The sideways assault was fairly common. You'd look to see who was walking in step next to you, only to be confronted by the sight of some sad purple rod peering out of the perpetrator's pants. Expecting the worst, I glanced first at his shoes, and was struck by the sight of huge red snakeskin cowboy boots. As my eyes traveled upward, I spied a brass horsehead belt buckle and finally the pleasant profile of a blond-haired man wearing a red ten-gallon hat.

I had encountered plenty of street-corner cowboys in Hollywood, some hustlers, some plain hicks, both young and old, but this one seemed somehow different. He looked earnest, almost sweet around the edges. He reached into the pocket of his black denim jacket and pulled out a lot of cash, neatly folded and clasped together with a gold dollar-sign money clip. He held it between his ring and middle fingers like Dad's friend Jimmy Black the card shark did when he was dealing a game. "I'll give you fifty dollars for a look at one of those," he said evenly, gesturing toward my chest, which, at the tender age of twelve, was an absurd C cup. I lifted my notebook self-consciously and pressed it tightly against the objects of his desire.

The outside bill was a hundred, the first I'd ever seen. I wondered if he'd give me the hundred for a look at both. We continued to walk side by side in silence, like old friends, as I thought of what I could do with fifty dollars. I'd take twenty at least and go over to Vogue Records and Books to buy a stack of records, for starters. I briefly entertained the idea of getting ahold of the money first, then making a break, but decided against it. This guy was six foot four or taller, and most of that was legs. He'd have me hog-tied before I could make it two yards. I also felt it would be rude on my part. After all, he'd made a direct offer, nothing outrageously crude.

Just then, two boys came racing toward us on their mongoose bikes, and from the corner of my eye, I saw my million-dollar cowboy pivot quickly and walk with giant steps in the opposite direction. "Is he who hesitates lost or saved?" I wondered. I had been ready to tell him, "Sure, okay, why not?" I knew that my mother did a hell of a lot more for fifty, and sometimes less, if she was up against it. I half hoped he'd show the next day, but he never did. I thought, with some shame, how appreciative I was of any kind of attention or empty flattery, even from a twisted stranger. Then I thought of Bunky's mom, on the night she came to our door requesting ice for a freshly blackened eye. "Why do you put up with it" Dad had asked. She sighed centuries of pain: "At least he's not ignoring me. At least I'm not alone." I must remember, I thought, to never feel that low.

## kissing the orangutan

When Dad got booked into the North Sea Jazz Festival, he sent me an airline ticket so I could see him play with other jazz luminaries like Dexter Gordon, Joe Henderson, Red Rodney, and Art Blakey, to name a few. It was good to see Dad earning some respect, even getting paid in the bargain, and enjoying the company of his fellow artists, who were the last of a dying breed. I remember sitting next to Eubie Blake and being hypnotized by his hands the whole time he talked to me. He had to repeat all of his questions two or three times, so mesmerized was I watching those long, lined fingers moving like hawks through the smoky air. Exasperated, he finally asked, "Honey, let me see *your* hands," taking them and turning them over in the awkward yet gentle way that old folks do. "Yeah—you're going to play piano with those fingers, just like your daddy." Though it was true that my E.T.-like hands would have found their way easily around the keys, I showed a total lack of talent in that area, much to my father's dismay.

While Dad was living abroad, he did his bit for international relations by romancing women from all four corners of the globe. "I love the broads I've met abroad," he'd sing while turning to catch the tail end of a too-young, attractive girl. There was, however, one notable exception. Her name was Berta, and she was homely, unhip, and quite a bit older than Dad. I'll always remember the first time I met her. Dad, Eubie Blake, and I were sitting in the booth of a nightclub when she appeared through the haze and stepped into the light of a baby blue spot near our table, which added to the ghoulish effect. Like some four-eyed dashboard tiki in a Joey Ramone wig, she headed our way with head bobbing from side to side. Dad nudged me as I turned to see him shrug and roll his eyes. "It's like kissing an orangutan," he whispered. I remember thinking that men were terribly cruel, and felt somewhat sorry for Berta, until I got to know her better. I quickly figured out that she despised me. She hated the bond I had with my father, and to spite my efforts, she was determined to be nasty. In her defense, the woman had narrowly survived the Holocaust and seen most of her family murdered. Whenever she spoke of it, her voice and body shook like Jell-O, but I began plotting her demise regardless. By the time I left for L.A., their relationship was on the skids. For my grand finale, I had "accidentally" broken some teacups that were apparently priceless, then denied it so tearfully to my father that he turned on Berta and called her a lying dog. Although distance and, in some strange way, success were slowly building a wall between us, the connection with my dad was still intact. Berta learned the hard way that nothing could come between a father, particularly a Sicilian one, and his daughter.

## homesick

The first time I went to Paris was in 1974. Dad and I were living in Denmark and took the train through Germany and Belgium. Paris was staggeringly different from the icy white world of Arhüs, Denmark's second-largest city. It was my father's favorite place, and when he exuded enthusiasm for a city, or a song, or anything else, it was highly contagious. We stayed at the Hotel Esmerelda. Mornings were spent hanging out our third-story window, drunk with sounds and the beauty of rooftops. Afternoons, we'd wander in and out of shops, my favorite being La Parfumerie. Inside its walls, a thousand exotic smells collided, and a vast collection of bottles, in lovely shapes and colors, graced the shelves like scented jewels.

I had no desire to return to bleak Arhüs. We lived above the bar where Dad was playing, and each night I'd lie in bed trying to fall asleep to the sound of drunken Danes singing along to the one same ABBA song on the jukebox. I loved the Danes. They were totally honest and open. It's no wonder they have such a high suicide rate. When Dad's job ended in Denmark, we ferried across the North Sea to England, living briefly in a dreary new town called Harlow. Fortunately, we weren't there long, and moved into London right off the Portobello Road. Dad was playing at a top-less bar in Soho while I experienced my usual difficulties making friends. English girls were the hardest of nuts to crack, particularly miserable and unapproachable. Dad had a twenty-four-year-old girlfriend who was living with us, and I began to feel out of place and homesick.

I realized that it was no longer necessary to protect my father from himself. He wasn't using hard stuff, and there were suddenly plenty of others willing to care for him should the need arise. People lined up to hitch onto his star, and I was a reminder of a past he fought to forget. I missed my grandmother. She had bad feet and ringing ears, and I could still be useful to her. When I left, there was an unspoken understanding that I wouldn't be living with my father again. The chasm that had grown between us deepened. Our goodbye was brief and silent, aside from an empty promise that we'd be together again soon "when circumstances were better."

With dreams of homemade ravioli, sunshine, and the wild irreverence that was Hollywood, I returned home to the sanctity of a world Gram had carved out for herself, and now graciously shared with me. For the most part, I'd have been content never to leave our apartment, outside of the occasional walk arm in arm to the market for supplies, and a weekly visit to the Tick Tock restaurant, where the food was soft and cheap. I could have grown old with Gram, falling asleep in front of the TV watching *Bowling for Dollars* in side-by-side ragged recliners with mismatched doilies on the chair arms. However, my other half attended school and concerned itself with the banal obsessions of youth. I had buckets of sand in both my shoes that needed to be emptied outside, in the hugely wicked world.

## the broken girl

I had a friend when I was thirteen named Kim. She wasn't the brightest girl, but she possessed a kind heart and many secrets. She lived with her family off Santa Monica and Western Avenue. It was one of the more depressing parts of town. We were in eighth grade together and got up to a fair amount of mischief.

She was the only kid who didn't laugh at my love of Busby Berkeley musicals. She thought it was swell, and I, in turn, did my best to be a companion in whom she could confide. Her father was as mean as a junkyard dog. He molested Kim's older sister, who OD'ed at the age of eighteen, and beat her younger brother, who erupted at fourteen and stabbed a policeman during an attempted car theft. He spent more time behind bars than not. Kim didn't give me the details of what her father did to her, but I gathered it was much the same. Her mother survived by turning up the Tammy Wynette to drown out the cries of her tormented children. Kim, understandably a dark soul, enjoyed sneaking into the Hollywood Cemetery after closing. We would shimmy right under the iron gate and commune with Douglas Fairbanks and others. "Here's to the great beyond," she'd toast, raising her Mickey's bigmouth. She could polish off a six-pack handily. I never liked to drink. Couldn't even stand the smell of it.

Kim had a bad habit of daring the fates to dish out more troubles for her. One Sunday, she and I were at Griffith Park when a guy on a motorcycle stopped next to us and asked me if I wanted to go for a ride. My intuition smelled a rat, and I declined his offer. He looked abnormally normal, and his smile was insincere. He was obviously not legit. He then turned his attention to Kim, who jumped on the back of his bike before I had a chance to protest.

No one heard from her for two days and nights. The police brought her home on Tuesday evening. The tragedy of those lost days was as follows. The guy on the bike drove Kim to a crappy apartment building on Vine, just south of Santa Monica, to "meet a friend," who was a second-rate pimp. The pimp handed the guy fifty dollars and told him to take off. He then tied Kim up and spent the next two days raping her in an apparent attempt to convert her into a whore by breaking what little spirit she had. Sometime on Tuesday, the pimp stepped out, warning her not to try and escape. She chanced it, and ran all the way to the police station at Cole and Fountain. The pimp was picked up and thrown in jail for a total of twelve hours before two of his "ladies" got him out on bail. He was never convicted for kidnapping, rape, corrupting a minor—nothing, as far as I know. The creep on the bike made a regular living out of picking up foolish, lonely girls and selling them like spring lambs to whoever he could for a lousy fifty bucks. The police gave Kim the third degree: "Don't you know better than to go off with strangers?" "What exactly were you wearing?" This incident was somehow twisted into my being a bad influence by her worthless mother, who forbid her to see me again.

I didn't see her for three years. I was on the bus headed for Hollywood High School when I noticed Kim, sitting in the back by herself. An unlit cigarette hung from her smudged purple lips, her hair was the back-teased victim of a bad dye job, and there were deep, dark circles under her too-old eyes. She looked loaded, and I didn't feel like approaching her. She pulled the bus cord for the Highland stop, and I waited for her to walk by before following her out. The bus stopped with a jerk, and two packs of condoms fell from the pocket of her dog-eared rabbit-fur jacket. I instinctively bent over to pick them up, then stopped myself. "Hey, stranger," I said uncomfortably, searching for a safe focal point. She looked up with her dark eyes and gazed straight through me and all of the world, giving a weak smile. She stepped off the bus, heading south toward Sunset, probably over to one of the motels around Highland and Orange that rented by the hour to johns and their hard-working girls, girls without much dignity to lose or family to speak of.

It could have been me, but it was Kim. What saved me was a crazy conviction. I had the idea that something along the lines of an all-purifying love did exist, in some corner of the messed-up universe. I hung on to that thought with stubborn determination. I wished I could bottle it and give it to all the beat-up, broken-down Kims in Hollywood. Kim died the following year. Gram saw it in the obits. Cause of death wasn't mentioned. "Are you going to send the family a card?" asked Gram. And say what? I thought. "Congratulations. All your years of abuse and neglect have finally hit pay dirt"? I let it go. There was nothing to do but let it go, and go on.

## the lamp peddler

I never had any desire to be a bad kid, despite my circumstances. I viewed shoplifting as an attack on big business, conveniently overlooking the fact that behind every store was an owner with a face and a wallet that I made lighter, as sure as if I'd picked his pocket. My behavior was at its dishonest worst when I was running around with a guy named Johnny B. At only eighteen years old, Johnny prowled the streets of L.A. like he was the only cat in the jungle. In his company I became a fearless and invincible thirteen-year-old, and feeling fearless was as foreign to me as it was desirable. He taught me how to hot-wire cars and run shortchange scams, which I did only once but still feel lousy about to this day. Johnny wasn't even from L.A. He'd started out in Queens and slowly made his way across the States, running one step ahead of the law. I once asked where he'd go if his luck ever ran out in Hollywood, which made him roar with laughter. "My thimbleful of luck ran out the day the courts threw my sorry ass into foster care. If I get busted here, it's straight into the Pacific Ocean for me."

The mere mention of the ocean gave me a sinking sensation. In the summer months, Dad and I had often ridden the Santa Monica bus all the way down to the beach and spent hours goofing around the pier or sitting on the dirty sand looking out. The vastness of the sea always triggered a despair in me. If I made the mistake of breathing too deeply in the presence of any endless horizon, I would burst into tears. It was as though I'd ingested pure wide-openness, and once inside of me, it turned into some huge, mournful creature. At such times I had a great need to hold on to something, anything tangible—seaweed, a sneaker, my father's warm hand. As if reading my mind, Johnny suddenly grabbed my hand. "Why the tears?" I looked at him with his black curls and beaten-up jean jacket and imagined for the first time since Alain that my heart was a blushing rose.

We were walking down Bronson toward Sunset en route to the plasma center, and there was a spring in Johnny's step, for in another hour or so he'd have the money needed to score, and he was happy. Sometimes early in the morning you'd see junkies and alcoholics in varying stages of need and decrepitude sitting by the side of the building, waiting for the center to open. From what I observed, they did little back then to monitor donors. Unless somebody was falling down sick and covered with tracks like 3-D road maps, they were allowed to give blood. Johnny joked that a great many people in at least twenty states probably owed him their life, for all the donating he'd done. "I like to give something back to society," he stated insincerely.

Johnny's crime spree would soon come to an end, as all sprees eventually must. One of his alleged friends had gotten a job busing tables at a place called the Old Spaghetti Factory on Sunset, and devised a ridiculous scheme that he swore would make money. The Spaghetti Factory had a huge, garish assortment of lamps that looked like they'd been heisted from a New Orleans brothel. This busboy assured Johnny that the management would never miss a few lamps, and he could make a mint selling them as Tiffany lamps to unsuspecting chumps. I was mortified. Even at thirteen, I knew they didn't look anything like Tiffany lamps, but this guy seemed to wield some power over Johnny, and I could say nothing to convince him otherwise. After sneaking out one floor and one table lamp, Johnny and I headed over to the senior center on the west side, where I watched in disbelief as he attempted to "work his magic."

"Hello, madam, I was just on my way to Butterfields Auction House with these genuine Tiffany lamps that belonged to my dear grandma—say, you surely remind me of her. Anyway, this is where she spent her final days, God rest, and I thought she'd like it if I first offered this investment opportunity to one of her, you know, own kind." This poor woman with her lavender hair rinse and slight palsy had been slowly backing up toward the door during Johnny's verbal assault. "I don't need a lamp," she stammered as she struggled to make her way inside.

"I need a new strategy," Johnny said to the lamp, as my female intuition suddenly set off blaring warning bells.

"Forget it. These lamps are crap," I urged, as he turned and snapped at me.

"Shut up. You're just some dumb kid." With those words, he walked away, pathetically struggling with the two cheesy lamps, and headed straight into a trap. It had been a setup from the beginning. The busboy had an ax to grind with Johnny, who'd been in town barely a year and "thought he was top dog." Together with a local dealer, they'd cooked up the scheme and informed the cops of the theft to have him busted. When this petty crime was added to the trail of troubles he'd accumulated in other states, he ended up facing a ten-year sentence. I ran home to Gram in tears when I learned the bad news. She had seen Johnny one time when I'd persuaded him to come up and meet her. Even though he'd bought her a six-pack of Lucky beer, one of her favorites, she had not been impressed. "Sure he's locked up—I gave him the *malocchío*," she said, making the sign of the horns with her fingers. "He's a bum.

You shouldn't hang around with bums." In the end, even if he had been more wary of jealous junkies bearing cheap lamps, it wouldn't have mattered. Once Gram decided to truly give someone the evil eye, their ill fate was sealed. As Johnny had noted after meeting her, she was "one tough old lady."

## flaming youth

Gram, having become convinced that I was heading down a thorny path littered with unsavory characters, asked my dad to take me for a month or so and straighten me out. Dad, the pinnacle of prudence and clean living, was supposed to redirect my wild adolescent energy into more sedate channels. He would have had better odds catching the sun in a bottle.

Dad was living in Amsterdam, which wasn't the ideal place to shelter your young from drug culture or sexual promiscuity. He seemed happy to see me, although it was an extremely busy time for him. He had two tours planned, three weeks in France followed by three weeks in Germany. I did my best to stay out of the way, help him pack, and offer him my enthusiastic support.

I enjoyed traveling around; it was a lifestyle I'd become accustomed to with Dad, even back in the States. We rarely stayed in one apartment for too long. It was a good way to stay ahead of trouble.

On one of my first nights in Amsterdam, Dad played at the Bim Huis, a great jazz club where everyone who was anyone played. It was here that we ran into Chet Baker, who was in a happy hashish haze, along with Dad and most everyone else in the place. I noticed a ginger-haired man with huge sideburns grinning at me intently from another table. Being a polite girl, I smiled back and thought no more of it until a note arrived from the guy, which was written in Dutch. I handed it to a Dutch friend of Dad's named Nils who was sitting next to me. After reading it, he crumpled it up, went over to its author, and tried to make him eat it. A short but lively riot ensued, and my admirer, who was no longer smiling, was escorted out. Dad, thoroughly engrossed in "A Night in Tunisia" on the bandstand, was oblivious to the incident. I pressed Nils to tell me what the note had said. "Oh, it was nothing, you know. He just said he wants to fuck your tits. Typical, right?" What a thing to write to a thirteen-year-old girl wearing yellow knee-high socks.

From the start of the French tour, I lusted after every young Frenchman I met, in every hotel and on every street corner. One day, while on the train from Lyon to Paris, I sat next to a beautiful French soldier who ran his hand along my thigh every time we entered a dark tunnel. The move was particularly bold since Dad was seated on the other side of me reading through some musical arrangements. Just when I was turning into a pool of fire, the soldier got off the train, winking at me and tipping his hat to Dad as he left. "People are really friendly here, hey Jo Jo?" Dear, sweet Dad. Europeans were now added to his list of people who would never harm me, along with clowns, dwarfs, and the rest.

Just as the French tour ended, Dad prepared me for the fact that I had to return home. "I can't put you in school here when I'm running around on tour, unless it's a boarding school, which I don't think you'd dig much." He was right. I'd have been miserable if I were institutionalized with a bunch of snotty girls. It was strange to see my father being so logical, so grown up. When I was little, he'd readily keep me out of school for an impulsive trip to the beach or the cinema.

Dad sent me back home, assuring Gram that he'd put me wise to the lowlifes who prey on young girls. Armed with this bit of ancient information, I returned to a place where I could make endless studies of a wide range of lowlifes—Hollywood.

## cracker

There exists, or at least existed, a certain reverse discrimination in the jazz world that's not often discussed, and I'll probably catch hell for bringing it up. It presented itself to my dad several times throughout his career.

In all fairness, African Americans gave birth to jazz and their desire to covet the music for themselves is

understandable, especially when it's compounded by de-
cades of oppression and deprivation. However, there was
a small group of white musicians, most of them sons of
immigrants, like Dodo Marmarosa, Red Rodney, and my
dad, to name a few, who shared a deep reverence for jazz
and had no interest in diluting or gentrifying the music to
suit the white masses. When Miles Davis made the stupid
remark that "White musicians play behind the beat," few
dared to protest it, many dismissing it as one of Davis's
"eccentric notions." Had the shoe been on the other foot,
however, such a remark would've caused riots.

I never gave any of this much thought until I saw Dad
play a concert in New York with a well-known drummer
who decided to use his immense talent to try and screw
up my dad's playing with overly loud, intentionally er-
ratic, off-tempo drumming. It was bizarre to witness. Dad
looked to him after every number, his frustration and anger mounting. At the end of the set, he confronted him,
and the drummer said defiantly: "I don't play behind any
trio fronted by a cracker." There was probably more to this
story than I'm aware of—some old, unresolved baggage
between them. Dad did have notoriously difficult relation-
ships with drummers. Whatever the case, he was genuinely
hurt by the encounter, though he didn't speak about it, in
great part because of the conscientious white man's guilt
syndrome. In the face of history, recent history at that, this
drummer's anger was certainly justified, but it was also, in
this particular case, terribly misdirected.

## blue lights

My grandmother collected eccentrics and madmen the way other grannies collect teacups. One such acquaintance was Benny. He looked a lot like Norman Bates and always wore powder blue cardigans, impeccably pressed plaid trousers, and white patent-leather loafers with tassels. The course of Benny's life was charted with the help of two spirit guides: one the spirit of a Sioux Indian chief, and the other the spirit of James Dean. He would greet you by grabbing your forearm with both hands, as if preparing to give a Chinese burn. He'd then hold on tightly, claiming this was his way of transmitting "healing vibrations" to the unsuspecting receiver. In the course of a conversation, Benny would invariably notice a little blue light shining over your shoulder and immediately shift his attention to the light, or "visiting spirit."

"Oh, hello, Jimmy. Nice to see you," he'd say. This one-sided discussion with invisible friends would often carry on for hours. At the age of thirteen, I was wound up tighter than a speed freak's watch, and when the blue light presented itself, apparently over my shoulder, I started crying hysterically while Gram scolded Benny: "Now that's enough! You frightened the poor girl to death." Benny, who called Gram "mother," would often ask, "Mother, do you think I'm gay?" to which she'd reply, "Goodness sakes—you're the only one who knows the answer to that question." Benny's companion, who he referred to as his "special friend," worked in the sheet music department at Wallach's Music City, and at Christmas he was the Broadway Hollywood's store Santa.

When Benny's special friend became terminally ill and suffered a long deterioration before dying, Gram watched Benny's well-groomed appearance and oddball exuberance die with him. They were two souls inextricably tangled into one. It appeared that Benny's spirit guides had deserted him in his darkest hour. Unwilling to accept the Christian party line that chalked up all human suffering as God's will, and too perceptive and sensitive to join the ranks of the totally faithless, he found himself in an impossible netherworld. So, like many before and after him, Benny plunged into the "bottle of forgetfulness," as my mom had once referred to a fifth of bourbon, until he finally drank himself into another dimension, where all his blue lights were turned off for keeps.

## princess bebop

The Auditory Blasters Club was a group of four nerds in my school who collected records of a certain sort, made tapes for one another, and had listening sessions at each other's homes on the weekends. Though "no girls allowed" was one of their strict credos, if loving music was the main prerequisite for joining, then I should have been a shoo-in. My one defining interest at age thirteen was collecting records. Everything from *Work Songs Live from Angola Prison* and the Stooges' *Fun House* to the *Pal Joey* soundtrack. Besides, I was Princess Bebop, as Dad called me, born of royal musical heritage, daughter of the Legendary Joe Albany. My ear was finely trained and my veins flowed with the bluest, most melodious blood.

However, their other rule, "You need to have a killer sound system to join," posed a problem for me. The club was apparently as much about the equipment as the music. These were all rich boys, all living in the Los Feliz hills, all with giant Marantz speakers and stacks of imposing electronics crammed into pleasant rooms with the obligatory rock posters and black lights. They looked down their noses at the kids who did drugs, like good little boys.

Rick, the most human of them, managed to convince the others to overlook my serious lack of noisy gadgets, and I was invited to sit in on one of their sacred sound sessions.

While listening to their rather dull ideas about what constituted "great rock," I began to notice that they all had abnormally large Adam's apples, and wondered if it was indigenous to the area they lived in or if it was a symptom of too much exposure to overly produced music or excessive money. After suffering through *Dark Side of the Moon* and *Layla*, which appeared to be a religious experience for them, I remarked that *Dark Side* was as overrated an album as they come, and that Eric Clapton was a boring guitarist. "His Yardbirds stuff didn't hold a candle to Beck's or Page's," I contended in my overbearing manner.

"I told you girls were hopeless," said group leader Dave. Rick looked at me, crestfallen and betrayed. "Do all of you agree on everything?" I asked.

"Some things are beyond criticism," said wise Dave as the others nodded in agreement, their Adam's apples sliding up and down their pimply pencil necks. Boys. So utterly righteous and ridiculous. I'd have no part of them for as long as I could help it.

## schoolboy hustler

Donny was a hustler, and he was a regular kid. His older sister, Christine, tried to raise him as best she could after their mom decided she "didn't like having children"—that was her parting comment—but at seventeen, after doing it for two years, Christine became tired and resentful, and though they still shared a room, Donny understood he'd be fending for himself now. He was fourteen, and we had two of the same classes at school, classes that the principal's son and the weather report lady on TV's daughter were both in too. Donny stayed in school with the hope of someday getting an athletic scholarship. "I'm going to be a great ball player," he'd say with a confidence that his desperate eyes betrayed. We waited in line two hours once so he could meet Willie Mays, who was signing autographs at Zody's on Santa Monica Boulevard.

Donny had a deal with a gas station attendant who would let him use the rest room for his johns, as long as he was added to the list of blow jobs. Donny was very matter-of-fact when discussing his work. "Pretty much, they only blow me. But there's three guys—well, I stick their dicks in my mouth, but they have to pay double," he said triumphantly. I was silent, which seemed to make him uncomfortable. "Hey, I'm no fag, if that's what you're thinking. I like girls. It's just—guys will pay. They always want it." I asked politely how he managed to feel "okay" with himself, since I was still suffering the tortures of the damned over the scene with my uncle. "Ah, girls," he laughed. "It's like—like blowing my nose or something. Sometimes I have to do it," he said, patting his stomach in a sign of hunger, "and it's over you know?"

Yeah, I knew. I knew he was trying to convince himself that he didn't feel like a piece of shit each and every time it happened, and that he could think all he wanted about baseball statistics and a nice place he'd call home some-day—but that at some point, the reality of it would eat a hole in him the size of a melon, and he might just blow his brains out if he ever let himself know what I knew. I hoped for his sake he never would.

I found myself often visiting the gas station where the creep attendant allowed Donny to have his self-respect sucked out, as long as there was a piece in it for him. I started stealing every stick of gum, soda can, quart of oil, cough drop, and car freshener I could get my hands on, hoping to somehow put him out of business. I wanted to kill all the bastards in the world who took advantage of hard-up, frightened kids, but I couldn't, so instead I ripped them off, conned them, and gave them the evil eye for what it was worth at every given and taken opportunity.

## no academic

Gram and I were now living on the corner of Vista Del Mar and Yucca in a brick apartment building that dead-ended by the side of the 101 freeway. It wasn't too bad as far as dumps go. The worst part of it was the manager. A middle-aged, broken-down Frenchman, he would slither out of dark stairwells and come up behind me, whispering, "I can give you more than those young boys you waste your time with." From that moment, I would never care much for older men, and would tend to gravitate toward guys a few years my junior, who seemed like a safer bet.

Anyway, the only boy I was wasting time with back then was fifteen-year-old Stanley, who sang in a terrible cover band and had burned off half his face attempting to breathe fire like Gene Simmons. We spent most of our time together on my roof, engaging in the awkward but energetic sex of youth. We didn't have much to say. I was covered in roof burns, scraped up on the small of my back and shoulder blades. At the fragile age of fourteen, I would've liked my scabby knees to have been the result of sliding into home base, not pointless sex with another lost peer, but there it was.

One day when I came home from school, I found Gram sitting looking out the window with an opened letter in her lap. "Is that from Dad?" I asked. She held it out in my direction without looking at me. I felt like a Gorgon. I took the letter and went up to the roof to read it. We lived in a small one-room place, and the roof provided me with some privacy. "Dearest Mom, It is my understanding that Amy is no longer a virgin. While she is certainly no academic, she is my daughter, and I suppose I must continue to advise her the best I can. I don't want her to turn into a rotten kid." He went on to write about some recording session that didn't register much in me after that first punch in the gut, and signed it, "Coraggio Mom, your son, Joe."

About two weeks earlier, Dad had gently coerced me into a telephone conversation regarding sex and what he casually referred to as "natural animal attraction." He then asked off-handedly if I'd done anything with my "little friend Stanley," adding quickly that it was "cool" as long as I "played it safe" and other such parental rhetoric. I fell for it, and decided to confess my sins of the flesh. Dad became suddenly silent, cutting the conversation short, and I knew at once I'd been a fool to tell the truth. What would he think, I thought, if he only knew of the others—if he knew of my uncle. I felt my face burning and looked high up through the clouds, concentrating on breathing, an exercise that usually calmed my anxiety. Now, however, it had the opposite effect, and I considered jumping off the roof, but at a mere three stories up, with my luck, I'd probably only break my legs.

I had to speak to Gram. Surely she'd tell me that I wasn't all that stupid or bad, and considering the lousy hand I'd been dealt, I was holding my own, wasn't I? "She's certainly no academic." That line would haunt me all my life. I ran downstairs calling for Gram, but she had gone out. On the kitchen table was a note that simply said, "Went to the store." So that was it. She and Dad were disappointed in me, to say the least. They would now avert their minds, and treat me like an inexplicable, unpleasant odor. I couldn't breathe. I tried to open a window, but nothing in that dive ever worked right. I decided to put my fist through the window. I needed a diversion, and it was the first thing that popped into my head. After all, I was no academic. When I punched the window with my strong left hand, a three-quarter-inch-long gash opened up sideways along my wrist. It was one of those strange cuts you can look right into, like an anatomy lesson, and watch all the little vessels doing a frantic dance in an attempt to heal the wound. Surprisingly, there wasn't that much blood, for the cut fell neatly between the two veins that ran parallel to it. I felt sick. Reluctantly, I walked down-stairs and knocked on the manager's door. He opened it, stinking of wine, and looked at me suspiciously.

"I've hurt myself. My grandmother's out—I slipped." He took me inside and cleaned and wrapped my wrist. He patted me reassuringly on the thigh. "You should be more careful, *chérie*—it could have been much worse." No, I thought, it couldn't have been. The person I worshipped had just cut out my heart.

## supernova

I succumbed to some nasty, unrelenting depression toward the end of 1976, and determined, at fourteen, that the time was right to kill myself. As I sat in my makeshift room, flipping through records, carefully selecting the soundtrack for my death scene, I began to feel surprisingly alive. My room was a two-foot-by-five-foot space, between the front room and the bathroom, that had a small built-in vanity and closet. Most old single apartments in Hollywood came with this dressing area, which I'd converted into a place where I could sit with my headphones on, smoking and wondering how to rid myself of the "sick-creeping-empty" feeling that had been dogging me all year. "You need direction," I'd say aloud, waiting for a light of perfect clarity to appear and lead me to an answer.

A few months earlier, a teacher's assistant at school named Mary had expressed a curious interest in my welfare, which initially roused my suspicion, until her persistence and corn-fed smile softened me up and I found myself breaking my self-imposed rule of silence, foolishly spilling out my most personal guts. We would walk in the park while she tried to make me listen to garbage like Loggins and Messina or Judy Collins, which caused me great mental and physical pain. Even in 1976, Mary was sticking to her hippie guns, which was endearing, in a way. She had a sympathetic ear and played the role of big sister quite aptly. One afternoon, she called to ask if I'd like to come over, with the earthy pretense of making candles. An unsettling feeling tugged at me, and I quickly declined her offer. After some awkward silence, she dropped a bomb: "Listen, I just think you're so sweet and pretty, I'd really like to make it with you." My first reaction was to laugh at her choice of words. "Make it?" Christ. She was lost. However, as the reality of the proposition dawned on me, my stomach tightened, and I saw red. I hung up, neither intrigued nor titillated, not even flattered, only pissed off that I'd once again been duped by some creep.

Later that week I bought a baggie of fifty whites from a boy at school, and now in my final hours I chose Humble Pie's *Performance: Rockin' the Fillmore* as my send-off music, for sentimental reasons. I'd had my first blinding orgasm listening to "I Don't Need No Doctor" earlier in the year, and knew well that it had occurred as a result of the singer's sexy voice, not the pimply guy I'd been with at the time. I could taste Steve Marriott's sweat on that album. While my unsuspecting grandmother sat watching the Jerry Lewis telethon in the other room, I began swallowing handfuls of whites, choking down about twenty before I began to feel them coming back up. My head was tingling and light as I started sweating buckets of ice water that smelled of chlorine. Then the sickness came, and came. I was on the bathroom floor with my cheek against the cold tiles, and I lost all sense of time.

When I was up to it, I dragged myself out of the airless, casket-size room and found Gram sleeping in front of the TV with the telethon still going strong. There was Jerry, and here was me. We were both freaked out on speed.

For the remainder of the night and through the early hours of morning I stayed up, overwhelmed by the feeling that I'd been both physically and spiritually cleansed. I saw and heard everything around me with an intense clarity. Each subtle change of light and even the most minute sounds were amplified. My skin seemed to be breathing as an independent entity. For a moment, I felt I had transcended the confines of my existence, and thought that my half-assed attempt might have succeeded after all. I wondered if this was how Dad felt, and if I too thought that the sensation justified sacrificing all earthly responsibilities. I decided it didn't. Perhaps that was the difference between us.

It had been a half-assed attempt on my part. I'd stupidly decided on speed, not wishing to die in my sleep on a quaalude overdose. I preferred to go out exploding like a supernova. Also, in my pathetic effort at self-parenting, I'd always promised myself that I would never use heroin, though it would have been easier. Somehow I felt that once I chose that path, I'd be forever lost. I still retained some hope, some interest in what might be. The "sick-creeping-empty" didn't have me beat quite yet.

## tragically unhip

When I was small, supreme contentment was listening to my grandmother's Al Jolson album. One evening, as I happily hummed along to "A Quarter to Nine," my mother, looking mildly embarrassed, commented: "Poor little Amy. She's hopelessly old-fashioned." It's always difficult to live up to your parents' expectations, and if your parents are the reigning king and queen of all that is hip, it's impossible. Since I wasn't listening to Coltrane's *Meditations* or smoking pot until the ripe old age of ten, there was fear that I was shaping up to be a real bona fide square.

The closest I ever came to being part of any scene considered cool was my brief foray into punk rock at the age of fifteen. It had little to do with the music. I was infatuated with a guy who called himself Bruce Barf. I met him one day on Hollywood Boulevard and was fascinated by his shoes, which were held together with silver duct tape. I followed him into an alley off Cherokee Avenue and down a flight of stairs that led to a club called the Masque, where he was a caretaker of sorts. I thought it was a wildly overrated scene, though I might have felt differently had I made some effort to talk to people. I wrote Bruce a long and amorous letter on the alley wall by the club entrance, which must have embarrassed him terribly, though he seemed to take it well. I started showing up at gigs there, keeping to myself usually and lurking quietly in Bruce's orbit. In the end, he wouldn't give me the wrong time of day, and I couldn't blame him.

My final disenchantment with punk came one night when I met up with four other people to go to a gig. A girl in the group looked at the loud pants I was wearing and remarked disgustedly, "Christ—don't you know that

Day-Glo is out now?" I glanced around at the others and saw that they were indeed all in black from head to toe, like a bunch of grim SS officers. Although I still went with them that night, the best part of myself turned on my heels, said farewell, and returned to the sanctity of home.

Punks, jocks, hippies, beats. The uniforms and the music changed, but the rules and accompanying rhetoric stayed the same. The most careworn hustlers and walking-dead junkies I knew still lived with some hope that the cold world and its diminished beauty would turn itself around someday, but these kids not only lacked hope, they seemed to embrace humanity's sad state. If I had followed suit and accepted that the world was nothing more than a dried-up cesspool, I would have died. I returned to my old-fashioned universe, a mad, unpopulated place where the possibility of love, above all things, fueled me on.

## danger zones

Throughout my life one constant, even in the lowest times, was my love of dancing. I thought if the world were to end in some cosmic inferno, I might still be content if I could dance among the debris. Though I enjoyed dancing with Gram or my dad, I was most fond of dancing by myself. Once a week, I danced under the trained eye of my instructor, Miss Lilian LaSalle. My free lessons (we were broke, but she thought I had great promise) took place in a church auditorium on Yucca Street. On one wall hung a sign that read HE IS EVER WATCHFUL, with a huge picture of Jesus beneath it. The eyes in the picture would follow me, no matter how much I attempted to dance out of their view.

Miss LaSalle had been good pals with Eleanor Powell, the queen of taps, when both were young dancers under contract at Warner Bros. She was an ex–southern belle from a long line of proud slave owners who still in 1977 referred to black people as "those coloreds." However, one could forgive much of her ignorance after seeing her dance.

Sixty years old, Miss LaSalle still danced like an electrified gazelle. An unfortunate accident with a bottle of peroxide had ended her career before it had really started. "We all had a platinum bob back then, and I was doing a touch-up—just the roots—for a screen test the next morning, when I got a blob of bleach in my left eye. It turned into this blood red that never went away." Her eye was a shocking red smear, and I couldn't imagine what it must have been like, to lose your career and looks in the second it took to squeeze a dye bottle. The pursuit of beauty could be a perilous endeavor. Being a woman of faith, however, Miss LaSalle seemed to take it all in stride.

One day she began our lesson with a ludicrous lecture concerning the female "danger zones." "Has your grandma talked to you yet about the three off-limit danger zones?" she asked confidentially. What was this now, I thought, anxious to do some dancing. She took my confused silence as her cue to continue: "The biggest danger zone is right here," she said, placing her hands flatly on her leotarded crotch. A queasy wave passed over me. "You must never let a young man touch you here," she whispered emphatically, bugging out her blue and bloody eyes at me.

I didn't have the heart to tell her that all my danger zones had been thoroughly plumbed by young men for years now. I tapped my heels nervously on the floor as she continued to illustrate the rest of the Devil's playground, the "buttocks" and "bosom" areas, and realized sadly I'd lost my zeal to dance for the day. This upset me to no end. I had great dreams of rising out of the ashes of my existence to become the pint-sized Cyd Charisse of my generation, and Miss LaSalle was now hanging me up. I interrupted her, complaining of stomach cramps, looked guiltily at the giant Christ, and ducked out and across the street with toe and tap shoes slung over my shoulders. I headed for home.

I made my way up to the roof, where I always vented my anger at the ridiculous, disinterested universe. How tired I'd become, trying to please hypocrites and politely listen to the advice of fools. I bit down hard on an abscessed tooth I'd had for months and was keeping secret from the world. The pain in my mouth exploded like a blessed distraction. If I could tolerate this, I could tolerate anything. I spit out a mouthful of infection and prepared to face the scene I knew awaited me downstairs.

My dad was here for a visit, which should have been a joy, but what should be, it seems, is rarely what is. For all three of us, Dad, Gram, and myself, an abundance of turmoil compressed into too short a time had worn us out. Like shell-shocked veterans, we were left wounded and full of doubt. Dad's reckless behavior now stayed confined behind closed doors. Gram, ever cautious and vigilant, became even more so. My own overwrought psyche made me increasingly dull and insular. I took my usual place at a kitchenette chair and watched my father nodding out on the sofa from an earlier visit to Lester Hobbs, who was still L.A.'s reigning king of junkiedom. Gram too was on the nod in her sagging green recliner, exhausted from battling the war she waged against old age. I sat watching them in numb silence. Gram suddenly winced. She also suffered with physical pain that she chose to live with silently. "What doesn't kill me makes me stronger" was her favorite cliché. I suddenly remembered a day some seven years back, when I'd returned home from school in tears, beaten up, with my lunch bag missing. Gram had looked at me and said, "What's wrong with you? Why can't you just get along with people?" The memory of it made me laugh out loud.

## old habit

As the years passed, it became nearly impossible for Dad to maintain his habit. At times, he'd stop using, but it was rarely by choice. He'd get busted or find himself flat broke, forced to quit cold turkey. Once when he was in his fifties, he attended a Narcotics Anonymous meeting. The man who'd lived by the words of Groucho Marx, "I wouldn't want to belong to any club that would accept me as a member," found himself in a large group of people half his age.

His "amazing constitution," which the doctors had often marveled at, was rapidly falling apart. With advancing age, he could no longer trade on the youthful charm and good looks that had once brought him credit with dealers and permanent loans from lady friends. Work became scarce. Even the hotel lounge circuit dried up, with jobs going to fresh-faced Juilliard grads who weren't likely to hit up the management for an advance or pull a no-show because they were loaded or their arthritis was crippling them. Dad reached a point where he couldn't afford to stay high, and the price of being sick was too much for his ravaged body to handle. A doctor sat him down and told him he was living on borrowed time: "Your spleen is shot, your kidneys barely function, and your liver is operating at ten percent. I can't say it'll help much if you quit, but you'll die slower." Tired of running the game, Dad found himself at an NA meeting filled with kids telling tales of hitting "rock bottom" that was grocery-line patter compared to his own life of pain. He then made an attempt at sharing one of his own stories. "I was busted for narcotics down South and sentenced to time on a chain gang."

"You mean like *Cool Hand Luke*?" someone interrupted.

"Yeah, sort of. Anyway, I escaped and made it to Tulsa, where I lived in an all-black part of town, passing as an albino, selling asbestos siding so I could make enough money to get home—"

He stopped, suddenly aware that he was being regarded with uncomprehending eyes. Who was this mad, gray-haired grandpa? What was he talking about? Dad excused himself and walked out. He thought maybe he'd gone to the wrong meeting. After all, they were all over town. No, who the hell was he kidding, what would he do? Be sponsored by some junior junkie who didn't know, hopefully would never know, what it was like to crawl around in life's dirty bowels for forty years?

Dexter Gordon once said that just after World War II, when drug addiction was largely a minority problem (he specified blacks, Italians, Jews, and Mexicans), the authorities didn't concern themselves with how to stop it, and certainly didn't care about rehabilitation. It wasn't until the sixties, when upstanding Anglo-Saxon teens, the children of cops and politicians, started showing up high for Sunday family supper, that the righteously uptight rushed to fight the dark drug demons. Where, in the midst of this sudden awakening, did an old, lifetime user like my father find help? The answer was nowhere. I'd seen it in the faces and heard it in the voices of health care workers everywhere. Dad and others like him were banished to the netherworld of methadone maintenance at best. "It's a young man's world," he'd say with a tired smile. I would hug his huge head, cursing my powerlessness and the futility of comforting words that fell flat and died as soon as they hit the air.

# the returning

Between 1972 and 1977 Dad had found a certain contentment living in Europe. He had cleaned up, recorded an album
a year, and, between jazz festivals and nightclubs, worked as
much as he wanted to. Like many other American jazz musicians, including his friend Dexter Gordon, he was shown
respect as an artist there that he'd rarely come across in the
States. However, the pull to return to the U.S. had become
strong. Dad had unfinished business to attend to here. He
never felt like he'd made it on his home turf, and now that he
had his chops, as he'd say, Dad was anxious to try them out in
the city he called his dirty, loveable bitch, New York. While
still in Europe, Dad received a letter from his old flame Jean
Roth, who lived in Manhattan. In it she expressed her interest in seeing him again, and enclosed a photo of herself in a
black bikini. It gave Dad the final motivation he'd been looking for, and he came back, moving directly into her apartment on West Fifty-Seventh and Eighth.

He'd first spotted Jean at the Three Deuces on Fifty-
Second street back in the forties and was knocked out by
her perfect, elegant profile. She had dark hair pulled back
tightly into a twist and long emerald earrings that ran the
length of her swan's neck, and sported the Nefertiti eyes
and red lips that were essentials for any hipster chick back
then. She was twenty-one, just back from modeling in
Paris, and caught up in the excitement of the new jazz—
bebop—that was breaking music wide open.

Dad and Jean had been together for a year or so before his habit outran her almost infinite patience and she broke things off. I'd asked if he was devastated when she left. "Well, I think the dope sort of anesthetizes you emotionally. I was hurt, but my relationship with drugs was still solid, so I never felt completely abandoned." Thirty-five years later, they were reunited, like some made-for-TV movie. Whenever I had the occasion to visit them during school holidays, I'd drag my poor father to CBGB or the Mudd Club, where he'd stand in back wearing the pained expression of a man before the firing squad, praying for earplugs to go with his blindfold. He played piano at the Hors d'Oeuvrerie, on the 107th floor of the World Trade Center, for almost a year, and complained that the crowds there were no more appreciative than the bums at the old Hollywood dives. Dad contended that the restaurant was always chilly because of the wealthy patrons who were "cold as ice, the way most people with money are." After a while Dad slipped back into using again for reasons known only to him, and he and Jean parted ways as they had so many years before.

I kept in touch with Jean over the years. She never had children, never married. She died of lung cancer about five years ago, alone in her apartment. In one of our last conversations, she said in her smoker's baritone, "Your dad was always the only one for me. I loved that son of a bitch."

# last dance

Children are fearless, their courage boundless. No longer a child, at fifteen I was a fearful teenager with a set of my own problems that overwhelmed me. Now that Dad needed me once more, after being kicked out by Jean and back on dope, it seemed unrealistic that I could take off just as I was starting high school and fly to New York, pull off his socks, tuck him in, and stroke his brow as I once had. Besides, I'd taken a weekend job, and the extra money it pulled in was helpful. Gram and I were living on $482 a month, old-age pension and child allowance combined. My job was going door to door soliciting funds for the erection of a new HOLLYWOOD sign to replace the dilapidated, grafittied old one. For a nominal donation a person could lay claim to owning a piece of the new Y, or whatever letter they cared to attach themselves to.

Before Jean broke off with Dad, she'd managed to secure him a small apartment at the Manhattan Plaza, a pretty nice building in a seedy area where musicians could live and pay minimal rent. I went to see him a couple of times. Each time I recognized him less and less. He'd grown thin and gray, slumped over from the pain of chronic arthritis. His eyes, which at one time had seemed to contain the entire cosmos to me, had faded into dull, colorless stones. Over the next decade, our relationship would be reduced to a sad series of 2:00 AM phone calls from Dad, sometimes pleading and at others threatening me to send him money

I didn't have. Much to my shame, the more desperate he became, the further I stepped back. I just couldn't do it. I wasn't even sure what "it" might be.

In 1987 a book of William Claxton's photographs was published. It included a haunting picture of my dad, and a nice mention from his old acquaintance Terry Southern in the afterword. I mailed Dad a copy, hoping it might inspire him. A few months later, in early 1988, Dad entered Roosevelt Hospital. I was on the plane going to see him when he died. At the time of his death, Dad hadn't seen my mother for many years, yet they'd end up dying within six months of each other—two meteors on the same collision course. The day after his death, while packing up his apartment, I found—among used hypos, trash, broken glass, and a shoe-shine brush I'd made for him at age seven—the Claxton book, sitting on the floor, still in its mailer bag, never opened.

## the end

Back in 1977, though I still retained a degree of hope for Dad and myself, inside I knew that ship had sailed years earlier, lost at sea with its cargo of broken promises and disappointment. Amid the chaos that came with my growing independence at fifteen, I still yearned for some parental guidance, which Dad was in no condition to give. It was then I made the decision to look up my wayward mother.

It had been ten years since I'd last seen my mother, and I found out from my aunt that she was living in some Tenderloin hotel in San Francisco. After tracking down her address, I headed over, full of nervous anticipation, only to find she wasn't home, although her door was unlocked. I walked in and saw two finches chirping blithely in a small cage on the window ledge. There was an empty pack of cigarettes and a beat-up paperback of the poems of e.e. cummings, with a recent picture of me that she must have gotten from my aunt tucked in like a bookmark. I hoped this was a good sign.

In the lobby I asked where I might find Sheila Regis, as she was now known, and was told to check the bar around the corner. Out on the street, just as I turned off Fifth onto Market, I saw a small heap slumped on the pavement. Something made me stop, for I had seen this configuration before. I went down on one knee and peered beneath the black bobble cap that was pulled low over a tangle of gray-red hair at what remained of my mother's once-fair face. "Can I help you, Mom?"

Her eyes opened slowly and turned to me. "You look like a slut," she said, with a vague smile, then simply closed her eyes and said no more. I kept kneeling, with one hand on her shoulder, taking in what she had said. I was wearing a pale pink shirtdress, the flat ballet slippers I always favored, no makeup, hair tied back. Had she looked into my soul? Did she know about the relationship with her brother and blame me like the rest of them? Oh Father, Father, where were you? I stood up and took three large steps backward—then jumped over her tiny broken body with one deft leap.

Fuck 'em all. It was the last time I would ever see her. I closed my eyes and never looked back. I headed over to the Mission, where I knew I could score some heroin from a guy I'd met while browsing in a record store. That night and for many nights to come, I would dive into the bottomless darkness of my life and sink all the way down. It was a beautiful drowning.

A. J. Albany lives in Los Angeles with her husband and their two children, Charlie and Dylan.